CUBA

101 *Beautiful & Nostalgic* PLACES TO VISIT

To Akiko & Nick — It's time
you come visit me in Cuba and in
the meantime I hope you enjoy
my Cuban explorations

CUBA

101 *Beautiful & Nostalgic* PLACES TO VISIT

best wishes & love,

Michael Connors

MICHAEL CONNORS

Principal photography by

JORGE A. LASERNA

RIZZOLI
NEW YORK

New York · Paris · London · Milan

CONTENTS

DEDICATION

Cuba lies ninety miles off the shore of Florida, and at 750 miles in length is the largest island in the Caribbean Sea, but it has been forbidden territory for Americans for more than half a century. For the rest of the world Cuba has been a travel destination well-known for its amazing culture, charming colonial towns and villages, immaculate virgin beaches, underwater trails, and uninhabited cays. The island has innumerable cultural heritage locations and historically significant architectural treasures, 263 protected areas, nine UNESCO World Heritage Sites, six UNESCO biosphere reserves, and numerous national parks. Cuba has much to offer first-time visitors, seasoned travelers, educated adventurers and environmentally conscious ecotourists, who are prepared to venture off-the-beaten-path and willing to explore the destinations in *Cuba: 101 Beautiful and Nostalgic Places to Visit*. While discovering the island visitors will experience Cuba's most impressive and important asset, the Cuban people. Meeting the gracious, resourceful, industrious, and hospitable *cubanos* and *cubanas* is ultimately the highlight of any traveler's trip to Cuba, and for this reason I dedicate *Cuba: 101 Beautiful and Nostalgic Places to Visit* to the Cuban people.

PREFACE

Beauty is said to be in the eye of the beholder, but it's a safe bet that no visitor to Cuba has ever declared the island anything short of gorgeous. Christopher Columbus, the first European to set foot in Cuba wrote, "Never have human eyes beheld anything so beautiful." He continued, "The country around the river is full of trees, beautiful and green and different from ours, each with flowers and its own kind of fruit. There are many birds of all sizes that sing very sweetly, and there are many palms different from those in Guinea or Spain."

I first visited Cuba in the late 1990s, on a trip to complete the research and photography for the Spanish chapter of my first book, *Caribbean Elegance*. Since then I have returned to this beautiful island more than one hundred times.

During that first visit I witnessed one of the most difficult periods in Cuba's history, ironically and euphemistically named the *período especial* during which the 1989 collapse of the Soviet Union meant the end of Soviet aid to Cuba, which consequently decimated the island economy. Economic depression became so severe there were island-wide breakdowns in transportation, and food was rationed. I found Cuba a place in crisis and in need. But I also found it an island with the oldest colonial heritage and material culture in the Western Hemisphere. In addition, and most importantly, I discovered the Cuban people and what defines the island's distinctive cultural essence, *Cubanidad*. Cubans are earnest and extremely proud of their culture and enthusiastic about sharing the island's history, land, and heritage.

Cuba: 101 Beautiful and Nostalgic Places to Visit is more than a mere book documenting a beautiful island, it is a guide to discovering, investigating, and understanding how Cuba's national and cultural identities have been cultivated over the past five hundred years. My most marvelous memories of Cuba are of the people I've met and places I've visited, where I immediately felt at home. This book is crafted to share those experiences of the Cuban people and places that captivate and haunt my memory; whether you visit Cuba or just get to know it intimately through these pages you will gain a glimpse of the Cuba I know and love so passionately. Let the journey begin.

INTRODUCTION

In the last decade of the fifteenth century, Spanish sovereigns Ferdinand and Isabella were eager to explore the Far East and exploit the resplendent riches Marco Polo had described centuries earlier, so they sponsored and commissioned Christopher Columbus to venture west. After sighting land in the Bahamas in October, 1492 Columbus set sail for what he thought (or hoped) was Japan—an island Marco Polo had called Cypango. In his ship's log Columbus wrote, "Then I shall sail for another great island which I strongly believe should be Japan, according to the signs made by the San Salvador Indians with me. They call that island Colba. . . ." On the next page Columbus added, "I want to leave today for the island of Cuba, which I believe to be Japan." This was the first correct spelling of the Amerindian name and one of the few native place names that has survived. Columbus first christened Cuba, "Juana" in honor of King Ferdinand's and Queen Isabella's daughter, but the indigenous inhabitants continued to call the island Colba.

Attracted by Cuba's natural deep-water harbors and the small amounts of gold discovered there, the Spaniards quickly began colonizing the island. The impact soon was massively destructive for the native population. Catholic priest Bartolomé de las Casas, known as the "Protector of the Indians," accompanied conquistador Diego Velázquez de Cuéllar during his Cuban campaigns and recorded the following in his *History of the Indies*:

> The Indians came to meete us, and to receive us with victurals, and delicate cheere. . . . the Devill put himselfe into the Spaniards, to put them all to the edge of the sword in my presence, without any cause whatsoever, more than three thousand soules, which were set before us, men, women, and children. I saw there so great cruelties, that never any man living either have or shall see the like.

There was an indigenous Amerindian resistance in Cuba and documented legend has it that the fierce Indian chieftain Hatuey was captured and burned at the stake in 1512 for defying

the Spaniards and rejecting Christianity. Hatuey's martyrdom has inspired generations of Cuban patriots. Under the auspices of having a holy mission to convert nonbelieving natives to Christianity, the Spaniards, armed with the "cross and sword," continued their quest for gold and silver through the Caribbean, Mexico, Mesoamerica, and South America. Within a century after Europeans stepped foot in the New World its native population was marginalized or exterminated, either deliberately and mercilessly or by diseases Europeans inadvertently introduced such as typhus, measles, influenza, and smallpox. Before long enslaved Africans brought to the region two additional diseases: yellow fever and malaria, the most dreaded illnesses of the colonial era. The consequences were devastating for the native inhabitants and more than three quarters of the population was wiped out.

In Cuba, the exploitation of African slaves began as early as the second decade of the sixteenth century when Charles I, who succeeded Ferdinand as the king of Spain, granted licenses to supply enslaved Africans to the Caribbean. Possibly the earliest instance of this exploitation and persecution in Cuba is described in Hugh Thomas's *The Slave Trade*:

> A few of the first generation of black slaves in the Americas played a part in the next wave of conquests. Diego Velázquez had had a few African slaves with him in 1511-12 in his occupation of Cuba, an island which would eventually develop a black culture more profound than anywhere else in the Spanish empire.

By the 1520s, Velázquez had established Cuba's first seven towns: Baracoa, Santiago de Cuba, Bayamo, Sancti Spíritus, Puerto Príncipe (now Camagüey), Trinidad, and San Cristóbal de la Habana (now Havana). Spain's slaughter of the Amerindians and quest for precious metals continued throughout the 1500s, and by the end of the sixteenth century it was said that the New World's inexhaustible supply of precious metals that arrived in Spain was abundant enough to pave the streets of Seville with blocks of gold and silver.

In the beginning of the seventeenth century Spanish thalassocracy had been broken by the English defeat of the Spanish Armada, and Cuba's production of any precious metals had abated. It didn't take long for Spain to realize that Cuba and the other Caribbean islands were valuable not for the gold and other riches that Columbus had anticipated but as strategic geopolitical and military stepping-stones to the wealth of South America and New Spain, as Mexico was called under Spanish rule. As a result, Spanish interest and priorities switched to exploiting the riches of Mexico, Colombia, and Peru. Cuba's geopolitical position, specifically Havana, became the most important safe harbor for the mineral-rich territories in Mexico and South America, principally because of the city's huge natural harbor and its shipbuilding capabilities. Havana Bay was the rendezvous point for ships sailing between all the Spanish colonies in the Americas and Spain, and made the island of Cuba the "Key to the New World."

PREVIOUS SPREAD: Sunrise overlooking the dramatic mountain formations (*mogotes*) in western Cuba's Viñales Valley.

My favorite cigar shop, where I've been purchasing the world's best Cuban cigars for years (top left) is right next door to El Aljibe restaurant, which is famous for its roast chicken. There are chess parlors like this one (top right) in every city, town, and village in Cuba, as chess is one of Cubans' favorite pastimes. The ruins of the great house (bottom) at Angerona coffee plantation (*cafetal*), one of Cuba's oldest, in Artemisa province.

Ships sailing between all the Spanish colonies in the Americas and Spain rendez-voused in Havana Bay. Spain's treasure fleets, numbering in the hundreds, would assemble there with gold, silver, and even luxury goods from the Orient and sail in convoy to Spain, believing that their strength in numbers would dissuade roaming and ravaging pirates. Spanish galleons, called Manila Galleons loaded with such Oriental treasures as lacquer-work, ivory, pearls, porcelain, precious spices, and priceless silks came to port in Acapulco, on the Pacific coast of Mexico. From there valuables were carried overland to Veracruz and loaded again onto ships, this time bound for Spain by way of Havana. *Habaneros* (residents of Havana) shared in all of these foreign riches well before the king, queen, and court of Spain ever laid eyes on them.

Agricultural products, namely tobacco, leather, sugar, and eventually coffee began to bring a new kind of prosperity to the island. The island's large landmass and fertile soil, a steady supply of seasonal rain and relatively few mountains made it a prime spot for agriculture. Europeans developed a taste for heretofore unknown tropical crops: maize, potatoes, tomatoes, cassava, chilies, cacao, pineapples, and tobacco. European dreams of acquiring riches in the New World brought about new economic horizons and the rapid acquisition of vast territories led to a large-scale transfer of population from both Europe and Africa.

By the turn of the eighteenth century Havana was more sizeable than New York and Boston and had become the third largest city in the New World (after Mexico City and Lima). Cuba's high-grade tobacco was the island's main export (sugar would later overtake it), and by mid-century Havana was shipping out more than eight hundred tons of tobacco a year to Spain.

Immediately after Columbus voyaged to Cuba, the indigenous tobacco plant was brought to Spain. At first it was thought to have only medicinal and therapeutic value. But soon tobacco became quite popular, and was well on its way to becoming one of the New World's most desired luxuries. It was said at the time in Cuba that, "Nothing is more important than tobacco." Tobacco constituted its own economic category of international commerce by the sixteenth century and Spain monopolized and controlled the commerce for more than two hundred years. Cuban tobacco growers became dissatisfied with the restrictive system in place, however, and ultimately rebelled in 1717. That was the island's first armed insurrection against the Spanish crown, and it was brutally crushed by colonial authorities.

In 1493 Columbus introduced sugarcane to the New World on his second voyage and established the Caribbean's first sugar plantation. As Cuba's agricultural production increased one of the harshest and cruelest systems of servitude in the history of the world developed. Cuba's agrarian wealth depended on and became inseparable from the exploitation of African slave labor.

By the mid-1600s there were as many as twenty thousand African slaves (referred to as "black gold" and "black ivory") in the Spanish Antilles, more than half of them in Cuba alone. Indeed at the time slaves accounted for approximately fifty percent of the island's population.

In addition to the Native Amerindian resistance there were slave revolts in Cuba, and during the colonial era these revolts were rebuffed violently and viciously in short order. The island's slave trade represented one of the largest commercial enterprises during the colonial era. In *From Columbus to Castro*, author Eric Williams quotes a late seventeenth-century explanation: "Everyone knows that the slave trade is the source of the wealth which the Spaniards wring out of the West Indies, and that whoever knows how to furnish them slaves, will share their wealth."

An estimated one hundred thousand enslaved Africans made the infamous "middle passage" across the Atlantic to Cuba over three centuries. At the peak of transatlantic slavery in the 1830s more than two hundred slaving ships sailed into Havana Harbor annually. Nineteenth century Prussian naturalist Alexander von Humboldt visited Cuba and described it as "the land of sugar and slaves." Enslaved Africans made Cuba's eighteenth- and nineteenth-century prosperity possible. While most of the Caribbean islands slipped gradually into a period of neglect, poverty, and decay in the nineteenth century, Cuba at the expense of enslaved Africans, continued its progressive prosperity and grew wealthier and more opulent. Cuba was the last Caribbean island to emancipate African slaves, and it did not do so until 1886.

Precious tropical hardwoods, tobacco, sugar, cotton, and coffee all contributed to Cuba's success as an island colony, and during the nineteenth century Cuba was no longer just a springboard for treasure-laden Spanish galleons returning to the mother country, but a wealthy agricultural productive island in its own right. It was especially sugar, the "sweet gold" that brought profits and prosperity to the island's plantocracy society. The *sacarocracia*, or sugar aristocracy, was responsible for making Cuba one of the world's largest suppliers of "white gold," giving it the distinction of being the "Caribbean's sugar bowl."

Cuban agricultural production spread throughout the entire island and smaller provincial colonial cities such as Santiago de Cuba, Trinidad, Santa Clara, and Camagüey begin to boast of awe-inspiring wealth. Havana's merchants, the plantation owners, and the colonial cities' shippers and traders continued to escalate and expand productivity and foreign trade, which increased affluence and created an aristocracy that demanded the latest style in architecture, fashion, and taste. As one author describes, "This kind of luxury was the norm on the periphery of Havana, where planters and other grandees had splendid manors, not only in the villages but also on sugar plantations, coffee estates and other properties."

By the 1830s, Cuba had not only become the world's largest sugar producer but the world's richest colony as well, and by mid-century the island produced six million hundredweight of sugar annually, more than twice the production of all the English Caribbean islands. Wealth continued to increase and with this wealth came the desire for Cuba's elite, both *peninsulares* (Spanish-born) and *criollos* (Cuban-born of Spanish descent) to exhibit their newly acquired affluence. This nouveau riche wealth marked the birth of a Creole aristocracy and the colony's

PREVIOUS SPREAD: In most regions of Cuba, sugarcane continues to be planted and grown by the same methods used for hundreds of years.

Cuban jeweler and artist Remberto Ramírez Oramas at his home workshop (top left). Guajiro (Cuban farmer) guitar music is an important and large part of Cuban life (top right). This Cuban family home interior is typical of what a visitor who takes the time to meet and interact with island residents may be invited to see (bottom right). The Internet is beginning to transform Cuba, and Cubans of all ages hang out in parks and plazas to use nearby Wi-Fi hotspots to surf on smartphones and tablets (bottom left).

architecture became more opulent and diverse in style with elements of Mudéjar (Hispanic-Moorish) colonial baroque, rococo, neoclassical, and beaux-art styles.

It wasn't long before native-born *criollos* began to resent the ruling-class corruption of the *peninsulares,* who were always quick to deny them any rights to self-determination. For example, a Cuban-born citizen was not allowed to bring legal action against a Spaniard, to travel without permission from the military, or be elected or occupy a public post. Most detrimental of all, a Cuban-born was not allowed to organize an industry or business.

Eventually this division of island-elites was responsible for the rise of a national identity and Cuba's Wars of Independence in the nineteenth century. Various wars of independence were fought in Latin American colonies beginning at the start of the nineteenth century and persisted until the twentieth century. Like all European colonial powers in the Caribbean, Spain governed Cuba with a greater emphasis on drawing revenue from the island than protecting the best interests of the colony and its inhabitants. Consequently, in 1868 Cuba saw the first of its three wars for independence. A planter named Carlos Manuel de Céspedes freed the enslaved Africans on his plantation in eastern Cuba and convinced likeminded planters to join him, thus triggering what was referred to as the "Glorious Revolution" or The Ten Years' War (1868-1878). In 1898, the United States intervened in Cuba's last war of independence under the auspices of protecting U.S. citizens and their property in Cuban territory. At the time the majority of Cuba's arable land was owned by a few individuals and corporations, many of them American.

The United States quickly defeated the Spaniards in a conflict that U.S. history books refer to as the Spanish-American War. While peace was reached with Spain, the Cubans were never invited to join the negotiations and participated only as observers. After three years of American occupation, Cuba formed its own government and formally gained independence in 1902. However the United States continued to impose restrictions on the new Cuban government. It reserved the right to intervene in Cuban affairs (it did so frequently) and establish a perpetual lease of Guantánamo Bay. Cuba was then governed by a series of dishonest puppet-presidents who catered to American interests via the kind of political corruption endemic to Latin American governments at the time that included fraudulent elections, bribery of officials and nepotism in political appointments. In addition, by 1958 approximately three-quarters of Cuba's arable land was owned by fewer than three thousand individuals and corporations, many of them American. This situation culminated in Fidel Castro's 1959 revolution.

For more than half a century, Cuban-American relations have been described as confrontational, malicious, and antagonistic. But since December 2014, with President Barack Obama's courageous initiative, there is a chance to heal years of strained relations. Finally, there is hope and both sides look forward to the future.

Overlooking the Bay of Santiago de Cuba from the city's fortress, San Pedro de la Roca castle. A seventeenth-century Renaissance structure that took more than sixty years to build and is today a UNESCO World Heritage site, it is considered the most complete and well-preserved example of Spanish-American military architecture.

CHAPTER 1

EASTERN CUBA

Cuba's CARIBBEAN *Cities*

Cuba has fourteen provinces and there's nowhere better to begin an examination of the island than in Cuba's eastern Holguin Province. Christopher Columbus came ashore here in 1492 at the Bay of Bariay, just east of the picturesque colonial fishing port of Gibara—a quiet, tourist-free, weatherworn coastal town with a trove of antique architecture. The name "Gibara" is derived from word *giba*, meaning hump, which refers to the Saddle of Gibara, a mountain in the distant southeast that historians believe is today the flat top prominence described in Columbus's log the day he landed. Gibara's Iglesia de San Fulgencio commands the main plaza, which is surrounded by picturesque colonial buildings painted white that has earned Gibara two titles, Pearl of the Orient and Villa Blanca (White Town).

Near Gibara is Guardalavaca (which translates literally as "guard the cow"), an area of gorgeous north shore beaches; among them is the two-mile diamond-dust white sand crescent-shaped Playa Las Brisas.

One of my favorite Cuban spots in this area is the secluded mountain eco-resort Villa Pinares de Mayarí with its chalet-style villas. Not to be missed are the majestic three-hundred-foot twin waterfalls accessible only on foot. A visit to the resort requires a difficult drive (a four-wheel-drive vehicle is a must) from the town of Mayarí through a national park, but in the end it is quite rewarding.

Holguín is the island's fourth-largest city and is known as the City of Parks because of its many shady plazas. It is also known for being a vibrant cultural center and the beer capital of Cuba, as it is home to several of the island's major breweries. A favorite panoramic view of the city is available by ascending a 460-step stairway to the top of the town's highest hill, Loma de la Cruz (Hill of the Cross), named for the large white cross that has graced the top since 1790.

About twenty miles north of Holguín is the town of Rafael Freyre, where the Velasco Cultural Centre is located. Designed by Cuban-American architect Walter Betancourt, the centre commenced construction in 1964, but wasn't completed until 1991. It is one of the few successful complete works of postmodernism architecture built after the 1959 revolution. It features an irregular-shaped central building and a continuous succession of roofed spaces surrounding it.

Between Holguín and Santiago de Cuba is the community of Birán where Finca Las Manacas plantation, Fidel Castro's birthplace, is located. The farm and house are now considered a national historic site and open to the public. A visit provides a glimpse into Castro's background and a sense of how his father, a poor Spanish immigrant, was able to improve his station in life and ultimately became wealthy by working for and with the U.S. based neocolonialist and exploitative United Fruit Company.

Halfway between Holguín and Santiago de Cuba lies the city of Bayamo. Founded in 1513, it is the second-oldest city in Cuba after Baracoa. Known as a hotbed of independence sentiment, Bayamo is still watched closely today by Cuban authorities. Its early colonial buildings were destroyed in 1869, when the townspeople burned their city to the ground rather than let it fall into the hands of Spanish troops during their fight for independence in the Ten Years' War.

West of Bayamo is the fishing and sugar-port town of Manzanillo, which stretches along the Guacanayabo Bay and has a historic city center plaza with an elaborate tile-work bandstand designed by José Martín del Castillo in the Moorish style. Many of the pastel-painted buildings surrounding the city square also have elements of Moorish architecture.

Less than ten miles south of Manzanillo are the ruins of La Demajagua, the sugar plantation owned by Cuba's nationalist revolutionary hero, Carlos Manuel de Céspedes, known as Cuba's "Father of the Nation." In 1868 Céspedes unilaterally freed his slaves, then invited his fellow plantation owners to do the same and called for open revolt and independence

from Spain. Spanish rule had become intolerably oppressive and the Creole class resented the authoritarianism and onerous mechanisms of taxation. This event lead to Cuba's independence movement and the island's first war of independence, the Ten Years' War (1868-1878).

Tucked into Cuba's southwest corner is the rarely visited Desembarco del Granma National Park. The park is situated in and around Cabo Cruz and includes the world's largest and best-preserved systems of marine terraces. Trails offer access to wetlands and semiarid ecosystems. The park was added to the UNESCO list of World Heritage Sites in 1999 and is one of Cuba's best-kept secrets for birdwatchers.

The road from Pilón at the edge of the national park to Santiago de Cuba is less than 125 miles but traveling the road is an all-day adventure, and the journey is one that a visitor is unlikely to ever forget.

Santiago de Cuba is a city that blends African and European cultures. That blend has created an exotic and intoxicating atmosphere; idiosyncratic not only in Cuba but also throughout the Caribbean, and a visit here is an absolutely unique experience. The city is known for its revolutionary spirit and the Santiagueros take pride in the fact that their city is called the "Cradle of the Revolution." The city's Revolution Square boasts twenty-three huge sculptural stylized machetes slanted in all directions and rising from a knoll. Created by the late Cuban artist Guarionex Ferrer, the machetes commemorate the March 23, 1878 date when Cuba's Ten Years' War pseudo cease-fire ended and fighting resumed. The machete was the iconic weapon during the island's Wars of Independence and the proficiency of the machete-wielding Cuban rebels struck absolute terror amongst Spanish troops.

In the center of Cuba's "most Caribbean city" is Plaza Céspedes, the main plaza, which is dominated by the Catedral de Nuestra Señora de la Asunción. Adjacent to the cathedral is the former home of Cuba's first colonizer, Diego Velázquez de Cuéllar. Built in 1516, it is the oldest house in Cuba and the best extent example of a colonial Cuban home. The house exemplifies the Mudéjar, or Moorish-Spanish, style that dominated early colonial Cuban architecture. (The Iberian Peninsula was under Islamic rule for nearly eight hundred years, beginning in the 700s.) Velázquez is an important figure in the city—he founded it in 1514 and named it after the King of Spain's patron saint, Saint James.

Directly across the plaza is the Hotel Casa Granda, and one of my favorite pastimes while in Santiago is to sit with a coffee (or beer) on its porch overlooking the square. The historic hotel was built in the early 1900s and has served as a backdrop for the work of many writers, including Graham Greene.

Music is another distinctive and fascinating art that is unique to eastern Cuba and especially associated with Santiago de Cuba. Numerous *comparsas* (musical groups) rehearse dance and music routines in preparation for the city's annual Carnival, usually held in late June or early July. Most of the music and choreography is based on the African-Cuban tradition, an important source of pride for the city and a product of the region's complex and

unique demographic. Don't miss joining a Carnival conga-line. San Pedro de la Roca Castle, about ten miles south of the city, is an enormous example of Renaissance military architecture poised on steep cliffs above the entrance to Santiago de Cuba bay. It is the largest and most comprehensive paradigm of military engineering in the Caribbean and was added to the UNESCO list of World Heritage Sites in 1998.

Further afield about fifteen miles north is the village of El Cobre. The Basílica de Nuestra Señora de la Caridad del Cobre (Basilica of Our Lady of Charity) commands the hilltop overlooking the village. This church is Cuba's only basilica and is the island's most important pilgrimage site, where thousands of pilgrims flock annually. The main attraction is a statue of a creole Madonna. Purported to grant miracles, the statue is kept in an air-conditioned glass case and wears a diamond crown encrusted with rubies and emeralds. Ernest Hemingway donated his 1954 Nobel Prize in Literature gold medal to the venerated Virgin. Other offerings include Olympic medals, Cuban sports jerseys, military medals, and signed photos of celebrities and sport heroes.

The road from Santiago de Cuba to Guantánamo passes through Parque Baconao, a park declared an UNESCO biosphere reserve in 1987. The road is dotted with archaeological sites, ruins of coffee plantations, mountain forests, and cactus-covered beaches. Teddy Roosevelt and his Rough Riders disembarked on one of these beaches, Playa Daiquirí, in 1898 during Cuba's last War of Independence, known to Americans as the Spanish-American War.

More than 170 *cafetales* (coffee plantations) are scattered on the rugged slopes of the Sierra Maestra mountains. In spite of the fact that nearly all the original plantations lie in ruins, some of the world's best coffee is still grown in smaller plots on the terraced mountainsides. The *Coffea Arabica* (coffee plant) was introduced to Spain during the 1600s and then brought to Cuba by Spanish monks in the mid-1700s. Cuban coffee production began in earnest during the last decade of the eighteenth century, when cultivated coffee seeds were brought from the neighboring island of Haiti by French growers fleeing the Haitian Revolution. Cuban coffee plantations sprang up in the foothills of the Sierra Maestra and in the valleys between Guantánamo and Baracoa. Cafetal La Isabélica is an example of the early coffee plantations and is well worth a visit, even though it requires an often frightening drive along a steep, serpentine road that winds around ridges and ravines.

Guantánamo is notorious for its U.S. detention camp. The lease between the United States and Cuba states that the base is to be used for "coaling and naval purposes only." So the U.S. jail is not only a subject of global condemnation and embarrassment, but a violation of the original lease.

The drive from Guantánamo to Baracoa travels one of the most picturesque stretches of road in all of Cuba, La Farola. This roadway stretches over the Sierra del Purial mountains like a beacon suspended in thin air; hence its name, which means beam of light. Remote Baracoa (La Farola wasn't completed until 1962) is Cuba's oldest city. Indeed, founded in 1512, it is the

The Quirch building with its minaret-like observatory tower is a Mudéjar (Moorish) architecturally inspired structure facing Parque Céspedes in Manzanillo.

OVERLEAF: One of the many ecological comfort stations found in the Cuban countryside for farm and field workers (left). Rice is an agricultural product that is currently being promoted throughout the island (right).

oldest colonial city in the Americas. This is the only region of the island where traces of Cuba's indigenous Amerindians can be found. Baracoa was practically destroyed during Hurricane Matthew in 2016 but has been rapidly rebuilding and is well worth the visit.

Ten miles past the gorgeously secluded white sand Playa Maguana is the Alejandro de Humboldt National Park, which was added to UNESCO's list of World Heritage Sites in 2001. Prussian naturalist Alexander von Humboldt, the father of modern geography, visited Cuba during the first decade of the nineteenth century. In 1826 he published a detailed account of his research, impressions, and experiences, *Political Essay on the Island of Cuba*. Humboldt's book covered a multitude of topics, ranging from flora and fauna to tropical climate, agriculture, population, and foreign trade. He is often referred to as the "second discoverer of Cuba," and the island's park named after him is a complex area of varied topography and considered one of the most biologically diverse tropical island sites on earth. It contains the Cuchillas del Toa biosphere reserve, declared an UNESCO biosphere reserve in 1987, and is recognized as one of the main centers of biodiversity and endemism in the country. Mountain fog forest, seaside white sand beaches, mangroves, and unspoiled coral reefs are included in the reserve. The area was also a battleground in the fight for Cuban independence.

I | BAYAMO

Cuba's second oldest town was founded in 1513 by conquistador Diego Velázquez and is famous for its long tradition of rebellion. Bayamo citizens (*Bayameses*) razed the town rather than surrender it to Spanish troops during Cuba's Ten Years' War. The interior of the house where Cuba's Father of Independence Carlos Manuel de Céspedes was born is a survivor of the 1869 fire and contains exhibits from the period. The nineteenth-century brass bed has ornate oval panels inlaid with mother-of-pearl (above left). The annual Fiesta de la Cubanía celebration with traditional Cuban dancing under the statue of Céspedes in Bayamo's Revolution Square (above right). The twenty-four-carat gold gilded polychrome carved wooden baroque altarpiece from Bayamo's cathedral, a relic of colonial architecture (opposite).

2 | PINARES DE MAYARÍ

A rustic eco-resort with large chalet-style villas makes the perfect base for hiking through La Mensura National Park, where the majestic twin waterfalls Saltón de Guayabo and pre-Columbian caves are hidden in thick pine forest.

3 | MANZANILLO/LA DEMAJAGUA

Gulf of Guacanayabo seaside fishing port Manzanillo and the nearby nineteenth-century La Demajagüa sugar estate that was owned by Carlos Manuel de Céspedes (opposite). Céspedes was the revolutionary who in 1868 unilaterally freed his enslaved workers and proclaimed independence from Spain when he rang the Campana de La Demajagüa (above) (equivalent of the American Liberty Bell) to mark the beginning of the Ten Years' War. OVERLEAF: A unique example of Cuban eclectic architecture, the Mudéjar (Moorish-influenced) rotunda brickwork bandstand, known as the Glorieta Morisca, sits in Manzanillo's main plaza (left). Also on the square is Manzanillo's Casa de la Cultura with its Spanish tile staircase brought from Valencia, Spain (right).

4 | CAYO GRANMA

This peaceful, picturesque fishing colony on a small island just offshore of Santiago de Cuba offers Mediterranean-style narrow streets and multicolored wooden waterfront houses built on piles with the owners' skiffs and rowboats moored below them.

5 | SANTIAGO DE CUBA

Santiago de Cuba is the most Caribbean city in Cuba and is considered the crown jewel of eastern Cuba. The octagonal mausoleum for José Martí (opposite) is one of Cuba's best examples of modern monumental architecture; every half hour there is a changing of the guard ceremony. A vast monument with two differentiated sculptures dominates Santiago de Cuba's Plaza de la Revolución (above). Cuban artists Guarionex Ferrer and Alberto Lescay created, respectively, the twenty-three stylized machetes and the equestrian figure of the nineteenth-century commander of the Cuban Army of Independence—the mixed-race Major General Antonio Maceo known as the "Bronze Titan" because of his physical strength.

The Bacardí Museum is the oldest museum in Cuba and is housed in an elegant neoclassical 1928 building that has become a national monument (above left). The Bosch mansion (below left) is located in what was Santiago de Cuba's wealthiest residential suburb, Vista Alegre, where other grand and interesting villas and attractions abound. Music and dance are a large part of Santiago de Cuba's life and Casa de la Trova, the former home of revered composer Rafael Salcedo, has become a haunt where local musicians perform day and night (opposite).

6 | PARQUE CÉSPEDES

From the sixteenth century to the present day, this park plaza has had numerous names and it is without a doubt Santiago de Cuba's most important social center. The Cathedral of Our Lady of the Assumption (left) was originally built in the early 1500s and has been rebuilt several times in the past five hundred years. On the same plaza is the sixteenth-century Mudéjar-style residence of the city's founder, Diego Velázquez, which is filled with Cuban-made antique mahogany furniture that is centuries old (opposite). **OVERLEAF:** Regarded as the oldest colonial house in Cuba, Casa de Diego Velázquez was declared a national monument because of its historic value as the finest example of the Spanish Mudéjar style in the Western Hemisphere (left). Santiago de Cuba's historic Hotel Casa Granda, with magnificent views overlooking Parque Céspedes, is the absolute best spot in the city for an espresso and people-watching (right).

7 | COFFEE PLANTATIONS

Ramon Guilarte's paladar is a favorite stop for home-cooked family-style Cuban food and is a place where the traditional process of making a cup of coffee from roasting and grinding the beans to pouring the boiled coffee is painstakingly demonstrated and enjoyed.

OVERLEAF: East of Santiago de Cuba is the UNESCO Archeological Landscape of the First Coffee Plantations in the Southeast of Cuba, which includes 171 old coffee plantations. At one of the best preserved coffee plantations, Cafetal La Isabelica, the house (top left), interiors (bottom left), and outside kitchen (right) have been meticulously restored and preserved.

8 | BASÍLICA DEL COBRE

The Basílica del Cobre is the holy sanctuary of the Virgin of Charity of El Cobre, the most revered religious figure and patron saint of Cuba (above). The triple-towered, ochre-colored church presides over the town of El Cobre (opposite).

9 | LOMA DE CIMARRON

This rarely visited lake is reached by climbing the seventy-seven stairs to overlook an old copper quarry now filled with rainwater, turned vibrant turquoise because of the water's chemical reaction to the copper once mined there (overleaf).

IO | GUANTÁNAMO

Guantánamo is the name of both a province and a town that reverberates around the world as a thorn in the side of Cuba and an embarrassment to the United States. Guantánamo's Museo Provincial houses exhibits that include the Russian space capsule that carried the first (and only) Cuban into space in 1980 (above left), and a 1940s-era Harley-Davidson motorcycle that belonged to one of Fidel Castro's most trusted revolutionary messengers (above top right). One of the art deco buildings in Guantánamo (above bottom right).

II | ROAD FROM GRANMA TO SANTIAGO DE CUBA

Although exhilarating, this road can sometimes be dangerous as it hugs the picturesque coastline with the Sierra Maestra mountains rising up directly from the other side. There are no gas stations or services, landslides and washouts often block the road, and detours are inevitable. An impressive experience one is likely never to forget.

SAN PEDRO DE LA ROCA CASTLE

At the entrance to the Bay of Santiago de Cuba, the Castillo del Morro San Pedro de la Roca is a medieval castle fortress built in the mid-1600s that was large enough to house more than four hundred soldiers (above). With underground passages and a drawbridge that spans the surrounding dry moat, the fort executes a daily *cañonazo*, or cannon-firing ritual, with military men and women in period costumes who stage the sundown ceremony (opposite).

13 | **PLAYITA DE CAJOBABO**

Along the southeastern coastal road from Santiago de Cuba to Guantánamo is an interesting stop where a white marble monument commemorating Cuba's national hero José Martí and General Máximo Gómez and where they came ashore in 1895 to lead Cuba's War of Independence is inserted into the Playita de Cajobabo cliff face.

This southeastern coastal road travels through both dry arid desert (opposite) and lush tropical areas where curious attractions such as these painted wooden beehives with active honey bees and organic honey are for sale (above).

14 | BARACOA

Baracoa (above left) is Cuba's oldest city and because of its remoteness it is the only region of the island where traces of Cuba's indigenous Amerindians can be found. Houses in Baracoa are interesting in that glass rum and beer bottles, many of them colored, are used as decorative windows (below left). Speleologists may want to explore the extensive series of sea caves that have yet to be investigated along with those that exhibit reproductions of pre-Columbian works of art (opposite).

15 | EL YUNQUE

El Yunque (the anvil) is the spectacular flat tabletop mountain that overlooks Baracoa and dominates the surrounding landscape. A hike to the summit takes about two hours and is well worth the trouble (overleaf).

16 BARACOA'S CHOCOLATE

Baracoa is known as Cuba's capital of cacao and chocolate, and one of the many attractions of visiting Baracoa is to sample the local chocolate, especially since it is organically grown. Although it is not known when cacao was introduced to the island, most experts agree that Spanish conquistadors brought it from Mexico sometime in the sixteenth century, and today Baracoa is the only region on the island where cacao beans are cultivated. To take the time to visit not only the Casa del Cacao museum (opposite) but also Baracoa's cacao growers and to experience the process of manufacturing chocolate from cacao is a rewarding adventure (top and bottom left).

I7 | YUMURÍ RIVER

The coastal road between Baracoa and Cuba's easternmost tip, Punta Maisí, is routed through a cleft-like passage and a tiny tunnel (above) emerging at Boca del Yumurí, where the Yumurí River cuts through tropically lush deep canyons (overleaf). Local boatmen offer their services to visitors for boat rides upstream for swimming and interesting ecology (left).

EASTERN CUBA

| **PARQUE NACIONAL ALEJANDRO DE HUMBOLDT**

This huge park (above) includes undiscovered mountainous rainforests, pristine deserted beaches, coral reefs, marine ecosystems, and the gorgeous Taco Bay. Just before the entrance is idyllic Playa Maguana, where the small yellow casita rents for ten dollars per day (opposite).

19 | HOLGUÍN

Holguín is known as the city of parks and plazas because of its scores of shady squares.
To have the best perspective of the city, take the steep 462-step stairway that leads to
a panoramic view of Holguín (opposite) from the top of the Loma de la Cruz (Hill of the
Cross), named for the cross that has stood at the summit since 1790. The city's colonial
architecture is characterized by its modesty and simplicity, but it also has fine examples
of art deco (above left) and other twentieth-century architectural styles. This young woman
sits like a queen with a crown on her throne atop the back seat of a fancy 1950s American
convertible with Holguín's famous bas-relief *Orígenes* in the background (above right).
Called Quinceañera, the Cuban tradition of a *fiesta de los quince años*, a celebration
of a girl's fifteenth birthday, marks the transition from childhood to young womanhood.

The magnificent eighteenth-century finely crafted cedar ceilings and the colorful baroque altar in Holguín's Catedral de San Isidoro make it an obligatory stop for visitors to the city (opposite). Next to baseball, boxing is the most popular sport for boys and men, and boxing gyms and rings like Holguín's stadium (bottom right) are found in every Cuban town and city. **OVERLEAF:** Fresh farmers' markets and roadside fruit and vegetable stands proliferate throughout Cuba's countryside (top and bottom left) and countless picturesque simple rural homes can be seen on every road and at every turn (right).

20 | PLAYA GUARDALAVACA

Guardalavaca means "guard the cow" in Spanish, a holdover from pirate days. Gorgeous beaches as well as excellent snorkeling and scuba diving are available at swank hotels with all the amenities, but there are plenty of isolated uninhabited beaches as well.

2I | BIRÁN

Finding Birán and what once was the Castro Ruz family residence (where Fidel and Raúl Castro were born) is something of a challenge. The two-story house was built on wooden pilings to shelter livestock underneath (opposite). The cockfighting ring (above) is still used today, and the bloodthirsty sport continues to be an integral element of the macho countryside culture of Cuba.

22 | BAY OF BARIAY

The West Indian woodpecker (above) is just one of the many rare and endemic birds to be discovered in Cuba. Others include the Cuban tody, the Cuban trogon, and the bee hummingbird, the world's smallest bird. A very small number of reconstructed pre-Columbian Amerindian rural villages can be found at various island sites. The Aldea Taína, not far from Bay of Bariay and Guardalavaca, is one of the most interesting, with actors costumed as Taínos recreating ceremonial rituals for visitors (opposite). The Bay of Bariay is most famous for being the location where Columbus first set foot on Cuban land (overleaf).

23 | GIBARA

The name Gibara (above) is taken from the word *giba*, or hump, which refers to the Silla de Gibara, the landmark flat-topped mountain (opposite) Columbus mentioned in his ship's log when first approaching Cuba on October 28, 1492. **OVERLEAF:** One of the many intriguing places to visit is Gibara's Natural History Museum, where a huge intact whale skeleton is displayed (top left). Gibara was the second walled town of Cuba (preceded by Havana) to protect the settlement from pirates and sections of the wall still exist nearby (bottom left). View from the rooftop bar for sunset cocktails at what once was a family mansion, now the Hotel Ordoño (right).

24 | SUGAR COMPLEXES OF HOLGUÍN

American companies like United Fruit Company created communities with the necessary infrastructure: schools, churches, hospitals, hotels, and theaters. Reminiscences of these communities surround Banes Bay and nearby Nipe Bay (above and opposite). The community called Central Preston that once belonged to United Fruit Company is today named Guatemala.

25 | CHORRO DE MAÍTA MUSEUM

For those interested in Cuba's pre-Columbian history, the archaeological-site-based museum Chorro de Maíta near Guardalavaca is an excellent source for research, and it displays a Taíno burial site holding more than one hundred skeletons (left), a gallery exhibition with an array of artifacts and historical data.

26 | VELASCO CULTURAL CENTER

The Velasco Cultural Center (opposite) is a formal, esoteric, and symbolic bow to what can be considered the typical economically disadvantaged rural Cuban town. Cuban-American architect Walter Betancourt, who called his building the "Song of Cuba," designed the center—which took twenty-seven years to complete after building commenced in 1964. It has since become a source of great local pride.

CHAPTER 2

CENTRAL CUBA, EAST

Cuba's AGRICULTURAL *Heart*

Camagüey, known as the "Corinth of the Caribbean" and Cuba's third largest city, is a historically and culturally significant center that was added to UNESCO's list of World Heritage Sites in 2008. It was one of the original seven settlements founded by Diego Velázquez and much of the domestic architecture corresponds with a combination of Renaissance, Baroque, and Neoclassical designs. In addition, many of the homes assimilate the Mudéjar (Hispano-Moorish) patterns and construction techniques. Named for the Moors (Muslims) who remained in Spain after the Christian reconquest, Mudéjar is the term used to describe the fusion of Moorish and Spanish influences, which is characterized in architecture by curvilinear arches and intricately carved woodwork, especially in ceilings and balconies. This Spanish

100

tradition of Moorish-influenced architecture brings an unexpected and elaborate Middle Eastern array of decorative characteristics and motifs to Cuba's colonial architectural legacy.

Another curiosity about Camagüey, and highly exceptional for Latin American cities, is the difficulty one has navigating the confusing network of irregular streets and dead ends, as the original city plan resembles a labyrinth. The narrow twisting streets and alleyways were designed to purposely confuse and confound the marauding pirates of colonial times who attacked and raided Cuban cities. As a matter of fact, Camagüey's city plan wasn't always successful, as some of the Caribbean's most notorious pirates terrorized, rampaged, and sacked the city. During the sixteenth and seventeenth centuries French corsairs Jacques de Sores (in 1555) and François de Granmont (in 1679), plus Welsh privateer Henry Morgan (in 1668), all made their way to Camagüey to pillage the city.

Paralleling for 250 miles the northern coast of Central Cuba's Camagüey and Ciego de Ávila provinces are a series of four hundred islands, uninhabited cays, coral reefs, white sand beaches and coastal resorts. In *Islands in the Stream*, Ernest Hemingway wrote of the area, "There was a long white beach with coconut palms behind it. The reef lay across the entrance to the harbor and the heavy east wind made the sea break on it so that the entrance was easy to see once you had opened it up. There was no one on the beach and the sand was so white that it hurt his eyes to look at it." From 1942 to 1944 Hemingway patrolled Cuba's Camagüey and Sabana archipelagoes, known collectively as Jardines del Rey (Gardens of the King) in his beloved fishing boat, *Pilar,* searching for Nazi submarines.

Access to the finest beaches in Cuba was made easier in 1988 when a seventeen-mile causeway connected the mainland to two beautiful contiguous islands in the archipelago, Cayo Coco and Cayo Guillermo. A third island where flamingos abound, Cayo Paredón Grande can also be reached by driving through the uninhabited Cayo Romano. There you can see a nineteenth-century lighthouse and fly fish on the flats to your heart's content.

Traveling approximately one hundred miles overland directly south of Jardines del Rey is the Archipiélago de los Jardines de la Reina (Gardens of the Queen), extending along Cuba's southern coast in an east-west direction for more than two hundred miles. Declared a National Marine Park in 1996 the access is strictly controlled. The mainland's departure point for the archipelago's best underwater photography, fishing, and diving is the small fishing village of Júcaro, where visitors are required to book passage on a yacht for a minimum six day diving and fishing tour of these more than seven hundred deserted and unspoiled islets and cays.

Even though Sancti Spíritus was one of Cuba's original seven towns founded by Diego Velázquez in 1514 and in the dead center of the island, it is the least visited of all Cuba's colonial towns and often overlooked. Of the many colonial features of Sancti Spíritus is the Museo de Arte Colonial, an eighteenth-century *palacio* that once belonged to one of the wealthiest families in Cuba. Another invaluable site to see is the well-preserved seventeenth-century Iglesia Parroquial Mayor del Espiritu Santo with its Mudéjar-style carved *alfarje*

PREVIOUS SPREAD: The Cuban countryside near Camagüey.

Cuba is the home of the *bolero* song, and *trovadores* throughout the island are easily found playing the guitar and singing traditional Cuban *boleros* (top left). This mahogany and leather lolling armchair, referred to as a Cuban planter's chair or a Campeche chair, is a distinctive Cuban furniture form found in every part of the island and believed to have originated in the eighteenth century (top right). The seventeen-mile causeway built in 1988 that links Cayo Coco, the Jardines del Rey archipelago, and mainland Cuba (bottom right). Yagua is the fibrous material surrounding the top of the trunk of the royal palm tree (Cuba's national tree) and has innumerable uses, from building rural homes to wrapping bales of tobacco (bottom left).

ceiling. Sancti Spíritus is also known for being the birthplace of the Cuban Guayabera shirt, and Casa de la Guayabera has a small museum with a tailor's studio and workshop where custom tailored guayabera shirts are made.

North of Sancti Spíritus is the small town of Yaguajay. The UNESCO Buenavista biosphere reserve is located on Cuba's northern central coast and is part of both the Caguanes and Santa Maria Key National Parks. This area offers extraordinary historical, cultural, and natural sites with thirty-five archaeological excavations and caves with Amerindian wall paintings and rural art.

The Valley of the Sugar Mills is southwest of Sancti Spiritus and known for the many ruins of sugar plantation and estate houses. One particularly well-restored eighteenth-century estate is that of the Manaca-Iznaga family; a nearly 150-foot tower rises above the property and offers sweeping views of the valley. Originally the tower was used to keep watch over thousands of enslaved plantation workers.

Both the Valley of the Sugar Mills and nearby city of Trinidad were added to UNESCO's list of World Heritage Sites in 1988. With its cobblestone streets, sixteenth-century Trinidad is the prettiest jewel in the crown of Cuba's colonial cities. Its colonial homes are painted in an array of pastel colors and still sport slatted wooden shutters, ornately turned wooden window bars, wooden grilles, and bands of hand-painted murals and decorative plasterwork on interior walls. If you can only visit one home, opt for Palacio Brunet on Trinidad's main square. On the same square is the eighteenth-century house (now an archaeological museum) where Prussian naturalist Alexander von Humboldt stayed in 1801 when he visited and researched the region. One block away is the Palacio Cantero. It has Cuba's most beautiful hand-painted murals and houses the municipal historical museum.

Trinidad has far too many interesting and beautiful sites to list, and the quintessential adventure is to simply spend a day or two strolling the streets with no specific destination to explore and experience all the unique paladares, museums, music cafes, shops, galleries, and meet as many *Trinitarios* as possible.

A short drive from Trinidad is one of Cuba's finest southern coastal beaches, Playa Ancón, where sun worshipers relax, swim, dive, and snorkel the nearby offshore reefs. On the drive to Playa Ancón is La Boca, a waterfront fishing village where foreigners never bother to stop and locals swim at the town's beaches.

North of Trinidad is the unspoiled landscape of the Escambray mountain range. Bamboo, eucalyptus, pines, palms, and ancient tree ferns grow alongside other tropical flora and fauna. Cuba's best hiking can be enjoyed in the Gran Parque Natural Topes de Collantes, a nature reserve park mostly unknown to tourists and a rarely visited mountain resort destination with its own microclimate.

One of the too-many-to-count serene, uninhabited white sand beaches on both the north and south shores of central Cuba.

27 | CAMAGÜEY

Camagüey is known as the *ciudad de los tinajones* (the city of large terracotta pots) because of the hundreds of antique vessels that still exist due to the excellent clay soil surrounding the city that was used to make bricks, tiles, and various building materials. The production of *tinajones* began in the late sixteenth century. The Iglesia de la Merced was part of the Mercedarian monastery, founded in 1601 (above left). The interior artifacts include the choir, Mercedarian catacombs (below left), eighteenth-century paintings, and a 1762 life-size silver tomb. Like most Cuban cities, Camagüey is a city of plazas and parks; Parque Agramonte proudly displays its equestrian statue of the Cuban War of Independence hero Ignacio Agramonte (opposite).

A colorful house (opposite). Located in Camagüey's Callejón de los Milagros (Alley of the Miracles), the Bar Casablanca is a realistic recreation of the classic venue where Humphrey Bogart and Ingrid Bergman immortalized their historic film romance. It has live music and stays open until the early morning hours (right).

Colorful bicitaxis lined up waiting for customers are always a dependable mode of transportation in Cuba, as long as you're not in a hurry (above). The Principal Theater (Teatro Principal) opened in 1850 and with its excellent acoustics has had a history of many celebrity performers, both opera and ballet stars (opposite).

28 | BAR EL CAMBIO

Bar El Cambio, which opened its doors in 1909, continues to be one of my favorite Cuban café bars where every Cuban rum imaginable can be sampled; it also happens to be one of Camagüey's late-night spots (opposite and right).

29 | MUSEO IGNACIO AGRAMONTE

This museum is the eighteenth-century birthplace and former home of Camagüey's revolutionary War of Independence hero. It is filled with Cuban mahogany furniture and paintings from the period, and the beautiful inner courtyard contains countless old *tinajones*, or jars (left and opposite).

30 | OFFICE OF THE HISTORIAN

OVERLEAF: The year 2017 celebrates the twentieth anniversary of the Office of the Historian of the city of Camagüey.

31 | JOEL JOVER

A visit to the home studio-cum-gallery of Camagüey artist Joel Jover and his artist wife, Ileana Sánchez, is an absolutely essential stop while visiting the city. Their home is a surreal and fertile visual oasis of art and worthy of a feature in *The World of Interiors* magazine (above and opposite).

32 | CIEGO DE ÁVILA

Ciego de Ávila was founded in the early 1500s, became a city in 1840, and today, even though few visitors ever take the time to stop there, the city is a compelling day trip for its Spanish colonial architecture (including the Moorish influenced or Mudéjar buildings), museum of decorative arts (opposite), Faith Pharmacy (top right), and the city's provincial museum (bottom right).

33 | PLAYA SANTA LUCÍA

This is the most famous beach resort in Camagüey province, with many isolated uninhabited beaches and others with amenities and all imaginable water sports (opposite); my favorite is the nearby white sand Playa Los Cocos (above).

34 | KING RANCH

King Ranch is a former cattle ranch with prize Brahma bulls, horseback riding, and rodeos with performing Cuban cowboys (*vaqueros*). It was once owned by the Texas King family (above).

35 | CRIADERO DE COCODRILOS

This farm raises American crocodiles commercially for leather (opposite). The smaller, critically endangered, and rare Cuban crocodile is found only in a few remote areas in Cuba.

36 | MORÓN

Morón is known as the "Rooster Town" (*La Ciudad del Gallo*). The present-day monument (above) was created by the famous Cuban sculptor Rita Longa. The work has acquired significant symbolic value over the years because of the centuries of legends that accompanied the previous rooster-like monuments. A nineteenth-century steam engine advertises one of Cuba's sugar cane museums (opposite).

37 | LAGUNA DE LA LECHE

Laguna de la Leche, or Milk Lagoon, is a few miles north of Morón and is named for a natural freshwater lake that appears milky because of the lake's gypsum and white limestone bed. Cuba's largest lake, which hosts aquatic carnivals, is a natural habitat for the Caribbean flamingo and is popular with fishermen, as it's full of royal tarpon, tilapia, and perch.

38 | LAGO REDONDO

Lago Redondo, or Round Lake (opposite) is
a short distance from Laguna de la Leche
and owes its name to the lake's circular shape.
Boat rides through the mangrove canals are
available (top right), as are guides for a day of
catch-and-release fishing (bottom right). Lago
Redondo claims the largest concentrations
of trout and bass in Cuba.

39 | CAYO COCO

One of the most beautiful small islands in the Caribbean, renowned for its outstanding and unsurpassed pristine beaches (above and opposite), the island takes its name from the white ibis, or coco bird. Besides its luxurious beaches, Cayo Coco is an important natural reserve for marine birds and is known for its hundreds of bird species, especially Cuba's largest roseate spoonbill and flamingo colonies.

40 | CAYO PAREDÓN

Cayo Paredón has the 160-foot Paredón Grande lighthouse (above) that rises majestically on the cay of the same name, which is a small part of the Jardines del Rey. Construction was completed in 1859 and it remains today as a luminous sentry that helps vessels navigate through the Old Bahama Channel, which Ernest Hemingway called the "great blue river." Flamingos are abundant around Cayo Coco, Cayo Guillermo, Cayo Romano, and Cayo Paredón Grande (opposite).

41 | JARDINES DEL REY

On Cuba's northern coast, the more than four hundred
small islands collectively known as Jardines del Rey
(Gardens of the King) remain uninhabited and relatively
unexplored (opposite).

42 | JARDINES DE LA REINA

OVERLEAF: Jardines de la Reina (Gardens of the Queen),
discovered by Christopher Columbus, is a more than
200-mile-long archipelago of over six hundred deserted
coral cays with nearly one hundred dive sites and is
considered by experts to offer the best snorkeling and
scuba diving in the world (top left and bottom left).
All-inclusive fishing and diving boats leave from the tiny
coastal fishing village of Júcaro (right).

43 | SANCTI SPÍRITUS

Deep in Cuba's countryside and agricultural colonial center is the off-the-tourist-track city of Sancti Spíritus. The pedestrian-only streets are easy to wander to discover the antique and historic character of the city and the most important sites, like the Museo Provincial (opposite and right.)

The town's oldest building, Iglesia Parroquial Mayor, built in 1680 (left). A religious altar (opposite) of Santería, a syncretic religion that is deeply entrenched in Cuban culture and grew from the arrival of enslaved Africans more than three hundred years ago. Slave owners prohibited African religions; consequently, slaves disguised their gods in Catholic garb and merged their homeland gods' identities with the Spanish Catholic iconic figures and saints. OVERLEAF: The majestic library, or the Biblioteca Provincial Rubén Martínez Villena (at left), and the Museo de Arte Colonial (right).

CENTRAL CUBA, EAST

44 | TRINIDAD

From both a visual experience and a cultural point of view, the colonial town of Trinidad exceeds all expectations. The river-stone cobbled streets and brightly pastel-colored colonial houses leave visitors with the impression they have been drawn back in time. Founded by Spanish conquistador Diego Velázquez in 1514, the town has a main plaza, Plaza Mayor, surrounded by historically significant buildings that were once homes to sugar barons and slave traders (opposite). One building was the home of Don Antonio Padrón, who hosted German naturalist Alexander von Humboldt in 1801 (above).

El Alfarero Casa Chichi pottery studio workshop has been owned by the local Santander family since the 1890s and crafts ceramics from clay found locally. It is an advisable stop for artistic and inexpensive handmade items (opposite). A walking tour, wandering, and even getting lost among the river-stone cobbled streets of Trinidad makes it easy to lose oneself in quiet nostalgia for Cuba's colonial days (top and bottom right).

45 | MUSEO ROMÁNTICO

Exterior of Palacio Brunet (opposite), a two-story mansion that was first constructed in 1740 on Plaza Mayor by the wealthy sugar count Mariano Borrell. The elegant dining area still retains its original hand-painted frescoes, fanned wooden *mediopuntos*, and louvered windows that filter natural light and allow air to circulate (above).

46 | PALACIO DE JUSTO CANTERO

Palacio de Justo Cantero was built during the early nineteenth century in the neoclassical
style and is an example of the verticality and voluminosity of Cuba's colonial-era palaces.
The palace's interior walls are decorated with neoclassical hand-painted murals by
Italian artists from Florence, Italy (above and opposite); these murals are found in every
room throughout the mansion. It is now the home of the Museo Histórico Municipal.

47 | VALLEY OF THE SUGAR MILLS

This is an aerial view of the great house of the eighteenth-century Ingenio Manaca-Iznaga sugar plantation, where more than four hundred slaves lived and worked at one time during the sugar estate's history (opposite). The monumental seven-level tower from 1830 was used as a lookout to oversee and supervise the enslaved workers (above). The plantation is located in the Valle de los Ingenios (Valley of the Sugar Mills) (overleaf).

48 | TRINIDAD RESTAURANTS

With the explosion of private restaurants (*paladares*) in Trinidad over the past few years, many cafés, family-style paladares, and more formal dining establishments have opened, and an abundance of gastronomical delights awaits those who venture out to find the best that Trinidad has to offer. A few of my favorites are Guitarra Mía, Museo 1514, and Vista Gourmet. My first-choice café is La Botija for a great cup of Cuban espresso or cappuccino and snacks (left).

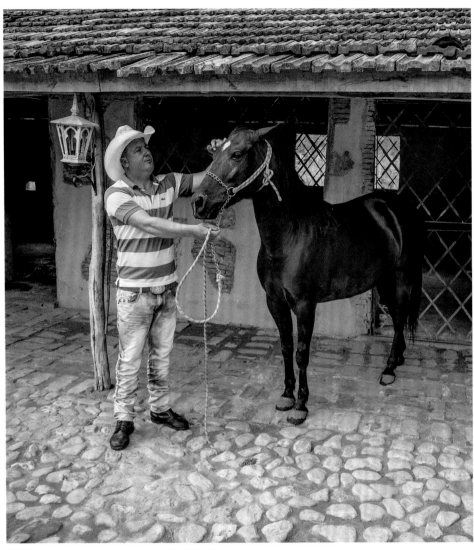

49 | CUBAN RANCHES

Taking time out in Trinidad is highly advisable, as the pace slows down enough so you never feel rushed. It's the perfect place to hire a guide and ride horses for the best part of a day for an excursion on the many trails available (above and opposite). These treks will take you through the Escambray mountains' Parque Guanayara and to the Caburní and El Pilón waterfalls.

50 | PLAYAS ANCÓN/LA BOCA

On the road to Peninsula de Ancón, approximately five miles outside of Trinidad, is the small fishing village of La Boca, where only the locals enjoy a series of white sand pocket-size beaches and fresh grilled snapper lunches (above). Further on is Playa Ancón, an enchanting three-mile sugary sand beach (opposite).

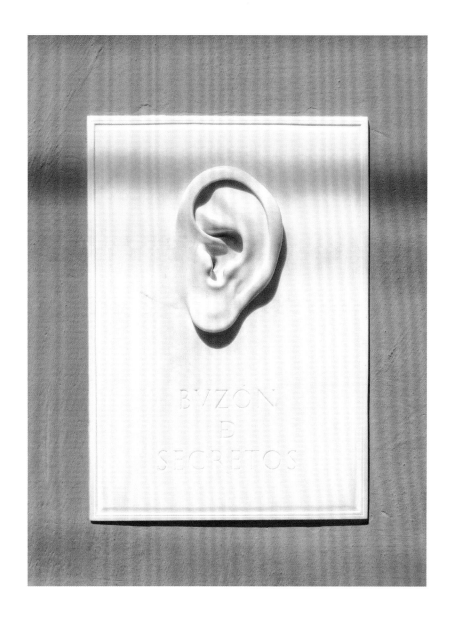

51 | CASA DE LA OREJA

The home of Trinidad artist Carlos Mata, who for years has specialized in nocturnal Cuban landscapes (opposite). Señor Mata welcomes visitors if he is in residence and his house is distinctive and easily found by the beautifully sculpted ear near the front door (above).

52 | COFFEE

Hidden away near Trinidad in the Guamubaya mountains popularly known as the Sierra del Escambray are Gran Parque Natural Topes de Collantes park and a little known coffee café where exceptionally good locally grown coffee is sold (opposite). Antique hand-carved wooden coffee production equipment and tools used for planting and growing coffee are displayed (above), along with archival photographs and local history.

53 | SENDERO DE GIGANTES

Sendero de Gigantes has access to the best hiking trails in the Sierra del Escambray area, which is home to some of the most dramatic and remarkable scenery in Cuba (above). There is not a trail that is anything less than fascinating and enchanting (opposite).

CHAPTER 3

CENTRAL CUBA, WEST

Cuba's COLONIAL *Cities*

On the road between Trinidad and Cienfuegos is one of Cuba's finest botanical gardens, Jardín Botánico Soledad. This approximately 230-acre garden features more than two thousand species of tropical plants, many of which are not native to Cuba. Edward Atkins, who owned a sugar plantation in the area and wished to propagate more productive sugarcane strains, created the garden in 1899. It was administered by Harvard University until 1961, when it was nationalized and taken over by the Cuban Academy of Science.

Cienfuegos was founded is 1819 along Cuba's southern central coast by immigrants from Bordeaux, and during the Colonial era the city was known as "The Pearl of the South." It is Cuba's third-largest port city and its nineteenth-century architecturally dramatic city

PREVIOUS SPREAD: One of the many *casas particulares* (bed and breakfasts) situated on the water in Cienfuegos' Punta Gorda peninsula.

OPPOSITE: Statue of José Martí (top left), referred to as the "Apostle of Cuban Independence" in Cienfuegos' main plaza. It's a short boat ride to the reconstructed Taíno village in Guamá near the Zapata Peninsula where there are twenty-five statues of Taíno Amerindians by Cuban sculptor Rita Longa (top right). The Zapata Peninsula is one of the few areas where the Cuban crocodile continues to thrive (bottom right). *Mamparas* (decorative glassed double-swing half doors) are found throughout Cuba; they help to establish privacy yet allow air circulation (bottom left). Music and dancing are second nature to most Cubans and can be found in many different venues throughout the island, especially Cienfuegos, a city with a great musical tradition and the birthplace of cha-cha-chá (right).

center was added to the UNESCO list of World Heritage Sites in 2005. The city prospered throughout the nineteenth and early twentieth centuries due to the deep-water harbor and nearby sugar plantations.

Cienfuegos is imbued with French influence, and its architecture is decidedly neoclassical and Beaux-Arts in style. One of the best examples of this style is the Teatro Tomás Terry, built in 1886, where world-famous figures such as Sarah Bernhardt and Enrico Caruso performed. One of the architectural oddities in the city is the ostentatious Palacio del Valle, built in 1912 by wealthy sugar planter Aclicio Valle. The building combines Mudéjar style with Gothic, Venetian, and Indian Mughal touches, which results in a mishmash of intricate arabesques in alabaster arches, Carrara marble columns and staircases, hand-painted tiles, crystal chandeliers, and carved Cuban mahogany doors and paneling. A team of Moroccan craftsmen was brought on-site to decorate the interior. Another architecturally eclectic palace in Cienfuegos with baroque, neoclassical, Catalan art nouveau, and Moorish elements is Palacio Ferrer, built in 1918 by baron José Ferrer Sirés.

The Bacunayagua bridge spans the Yumurí river in Matanzas province and at the lookout point with breathtaking views the piña coladas are served in pineapples (opposite). The Club Cienfuegos served as the city's yacht club until the 1959 revolution and today still exhibits antique silver yachting trophies and maritime memorabilia. Sailboats can be rented for sailing around Cienfuegos Bay (below).

East of Cienfuegos is the Ciénaga de Zapata biosphere reserve, the largest and most pristine wetlands in the Caribbean. It is an unparalleled refuge for rare birds, such as neon pink flamingos and spoonbills. Both the rare and endangered Cuban crocodile and the more common American crocodile sun themselves on the mudflats. This UNESCO biosphere reserve was designated in 2000 and placed on the RAMSAR list (Wetlands of International Importance) in 2001. It is noted for its endless grasslands and mangroves, together with a coastline of lagoons, small islands, and keys surrounded by unspoiled live coral reefs.

Located between Cienfuegos and Remedios is the city of Santa Clara, best known today for its monuments to Che Guevara, the Marxist revolutionary Argentine who fought alongside Fidel Castro to topple the Fulgencio Batista regime. Santa Clara was founded in 1689 by a group of residents of Remedios who ventured further inland to escape the constant

pirate raids in their coastal town. One of the highlights of Santa Clara is the Museo de Artes Decorativas, a museum which offers an extensive collection of eighteenth- and nineteenth-century Cuban furniture, paintings, porcelain, and objets d'art.

The charming colonial town of Remedios, about thirty miles northeast of Santa Clara, is worth a visit any time of year, but on December 24th it really shines with Las Parrandas, an annual festival that continues a two-hundred-year-old tradition of what has been described as "pyrotechnic insanity." Rum flows freely as elaborately decorated lantern-lit floats with costumed dancers, musicians, and performers compete for attention. The evening culminates in displays of fireworks and homemade rockets that light up the night and early morning skies for hours. A local museum dedicated to the festival features photographs, costumes, small decorated floats, and homemade rockets. Also in Remedios, the seventeenth-century Parroquia de San Juan Bautista church contains a lavish Churrigueresque altar carved from cedar and encrusted with twenty-four-carat gold leaf, as well as a fluted and gabled Mudéjar-style mahogany ceiling.

Matanzas was founded in the late seventeenth century and built overlooking the deep-water bay of the same name. It has long been known as the "Athens of Cuba" because during the nineteenth century its artistic and cultural life shone brighter than in any other Cuban city. It has been a cultural leader in the latest fashions of music, dance, architecture, and theater. The city's neoclassical opera theatre, Teatro Sauto, was built in 1863. Under restoration at the time of this writing it promises once again to be the prestigious cultural institution it was 150 years ago. One of the city's most famous legacies from the nineteenth century is Cuba's musical genre, danzón, a combination of classical music and African rhythms. This Creole and Caribbean adaptation of European country dancing was born in 1879 composed by Matanzas bandleader, Miguel Failde, and it became the most popular dance in Cuba for more than fifty years and even now is practiced at the Casa de Danzón near Plaza de la Vigia. Not far away on Plaza de la Libertad is Cuba's finest example of an original nineteenth-century pharmacy, built in 1882 by French pharmacist Ernest Triolet; today it is named the Museo Farmacéutico and is the most complete pharmaceutical museum in the Americas.

The beach community of Varadero occupies the twelve-mile long Hicacos peninsula, which is lined with a series of white sand beaches. It is connected to the mainland by a drawbridge. Varadero is no secret—it is Cuba's most popular beach resort and a destination for both foreign tourists and Cubans. But many come simply to enjoy the (admittedly gorgeous) beaches and miss out on the interesting places to visit. These include the beachfront Spanish-style Mansión Xanadú, built in 1926 by American millionaire Irénée du Pont and used as a family vacation home until 1960, when it was nationalized by the Cuban government and transformed into a small six-room hotel, restaurant, and clubhouse. Another interesting stop is the local municipal museum, housed in a classic 1920s wooden vacation home on the beach.

The pristine white sand beaches of Varadero are world renowned and it has a reputation for being the best area in Cuba for watersports enthusiasts.

54 | **CIENFUEGOS BAY**

The naturally well-protected bay of Cienfuegos was one of Cuba's chief seaports and the center of the sugar trade as well as the tobacco and coffee trades during the nineteenth century and the first half of the twentieth century. The American schooner *Harvey Gamage* is at anchor in Cienfuegos Bay (above). A view from the water of a typical waterfront house along the Punta Gorda peninsula at the southern tip of Cienfuegos Bay (opposite).

55 | CIENFUEGOS

This city is known as Cuba's "Pearl of the South" and was settled mostly by French immigrants during the colonial era in the early 1800s. The late Cuban singer, songwriter, and bandleader Benny Moré is Cienfuegos' most celebrated resident and is depicted on the city's welcoming sign, which reads, "Cienfuegos is the city that I like the most," lyrics to the song Moré composed and dedicated to the city (opposite). One of the many attractions in Cienfuegos is the National Museum of Naval History and its collection of naval warfare and seafaring exhibits (above). **OVERLEAF**: Teatro Tomás Terry (left) was built in 1886 and designed as an Italian-style theater with a U-shaped two-tiered auditorium and a gorgeous ceiling fresco by Camilo Salaya, a Filipino-Spanish painter. World-famous figures such as Sarah Bernhardt and Enrico Caruso performed here. The ostentation and decidedly Mudéjar influence of Palacio del Valle on Punta Gorda reflects the vast fortune acquired by sugar planter Aclicio Valle, who built the mansion in 1912. Today it is a bar and restaurant (right).

Por acercar el hombre a la naturaleza

Jardín Botánico de Cienfuegos

56 | JARDÍN BOTÁNICO DE CIENFUEGOS

Just ten miles from the city, this botanical garden has the most extensive collection of tropical plants in Cuba. It was founded in 1901 by American Edwin Atkins and has been run by the Cuban government since 1961 (opposite).

57 | CIÉNAGA DE ZAPATA

The Zapata swamp located on the Zapata Peninsula is a national park and UNESCO biosphere reserve and is the most complete wildlife reserve in Cuba. Of the innumerable activities, trekking, watersports, bird-watching, fishing, and visiting the reconstructed Taíno Amerindian village on the lake are greatly recommended (right and overleaf).

58 | REMEDIOS

Remedios is one of the oldest towns in Cuba and aside from hosting Cuba's biggest fireworks festival, Las Parrandas, on Christmas Eve, the stunning Iglesia de San Juan Bautista church (top right) displays Cuba's most elegant altar. The seventeenth-century carved cedar Churrigueresque-style, twenty-four-carat gold altarpiece is topped by the Mudéjar (Moorish) style cedar and mahogany ceiling typical of early Cuban craftsmanship (opposite). Hotel Camino del Príncipe is representative of the colonial architecture in Remedios (bottom right).

59 | SANTA CLARA

OVERLEAF: Interiors of the palacio of a prominent nineteenth-century family built in 1810. Filled with period furniture and objets d'art, today it is the city's Museum of Decorative Arts.

60 | CÁRDENAS

One of the least visited colonial cities on the island offers a taste of Cuban life without foreign tourists and with horse-drawn carriages as the main means of transportation. It is known for its many elaborate carriages that substitute for taxis (opposite). An extremely elaborate and grandiose carriage, a nineteenth-century baroque horse-drawn hearse, can be seen in the Oscar María de Rojas Museum (top and bottom right).

61 | MATANZAS

OVERLEAF: Matanzas is another Cuban city infrequently visited by foreign tourists and it holds hidden surprises around every corner. Situated on the shores of Matanzas Bay, the preponderance of nineteenth-century neoclassical architecture is significant; even the city's fire station is a model of the neoclassical style (right). A visit to Matanzas isn't complete without stopping in to see the handcrafted books and publishing products displayed (some are for sale) at Ediciones Vigía (bottom left). A trip to the Museum of Decorative Arts (top left) and Sauto Theater should be added to any visitor´s itinerary.

195

62 | MUSEO FARMACÉUTICO

The finest example of an original nineteenth-century pharmacy in the Western Hemisphere can be seen in Matanzas. It was built in the 1880s by French pharmacist Ernest Triolet. The Cuban mahogany cabinets and shelves store the original hand-decorated French porcelain vases and jars (left).

63 | VARADERO

An example of the many early wooden chalet-style beachside vacation homes with delicate fretwork and French roof tiles that were built by wealthy Cubans at the turn of the twentieth century in Varadero, the largest seaside resort in Cuba today (opposite). **OVERLEAF:** The beachfront Spanish-style six bedroom mansion named Xanadú, built in 1926 by American millionaire Irénée du Pont, served as a family vacation home and is today a boutique hotel and restaurant.

CHAPTER 4

WESTERN CUBA

Cuba's TOBACCO *Bowl*

Pinar del Río is Cuba's westernmost province, and the province's largest city with the same name is 110 miles west of Havana. No trip to Cuba would be complete without making the two-hour drive to visit the town of Pinar del Río and the surrounding countryside, best known for Valle de Viñales (Viñales Valley) and its endless emblematic cultivated tobacco fields. The Viñales Valley was added to UNESCO's World Heritage sites in 1999 and its unique landscape contains gigantic limestone karst formations that look like haystacks. Often covered with a morning mist, these limestone *mogotes* are among the most ancient rock configurations in Cuba and are one of the most beautiful sites on the entire island.

PREVIOUS SPREAD: Western Cuba's farmers continue to till tobacco fields with ox-drawn plows as they did hundreds of years ago.

The antique train station at Herradura in Cuba's western province of Pinar del Río, where an American community was founded as part of the failed adventure of U.S. colonies in Cuba during the first thirty years of the 1900s (top left). Rachel García, owner of Finca Agroecológica El Paraíso, unquestionably the best *paladar* in the Pinar del Río province (top right). One of the thousands of orchids at Soroa Orchid Garden, located between Pinar del Río and Havana (bottom right). A hand-crafted wooden coffee grinding device found at the Buenavista coffee plantation (bottom left).

OVERLEAF: Painted on one the Viñales Valley *mogotes,* this controversial illustration represents the evolution of the area's inhabitants from sea mollusks and dinosaurs to humans. The mural measures more than 200 feet high and 300 feet wide and, although considered by most to be in poor taste, continues to be a favorite subject for photographers.

A short distance away from the city of Pinar del Río is the distinctly nineteenth-century town of Viñales with newly and brightly painted, red-tiled roofed houses many of which are now advertising rooms for rent to visitors. Elegant and impressive pine trees line the main street, Calle Salvador Cisneros, where backpackers roam looking for the nearest paladar to eat or *casa particular* to stay the night. My favorite paladar in the area is Rachel Garcia's Finca Agroecológica El Paraíso, where one is served family-style an array of delicious Cuban dishes. Rachel's secret-recipe piña colada and her roast pork dish are not to be missed.

Off the beaten path and hidden among the *mogotes* (hills) are numerous forgotten caves and valleys waiting to be explored, the most secret of which involves a thirty-minute hike through Valle del Ancon to a concealed cave, after which a twenty-minute trek through the cave brings one to the Valle Ruiseñor. This valley is locally known as Valle del Silencio (Silent or Secret Valley) and is accessible only through Valle del Ancon's small secluded and camouflaged cave entrance. The valley will remind visitors who make the hike of Jurassic Park devoid of dinosaurs.

The area is as well known for its countless tobacco fields as it is for Viñales Valley and a visitor never escapes the ubiquitous aroma of tobacco. The world's best tobacco is grown in this area where oxen still plow the fields in preparation for seeding and the tobacco leaves are still hand picked. Cuba has always been the exportation capital of tobacco and traditional techniques handed down over the past two hundred years have been continually practiced for its cultivation and production. It's important to remember that the tobacco plant is indigenous to the island and was smoked by the Amerindians. It was brought back to Spain where it not only gained popularity in Spain but with the entire New World Empire and European aristocrats.

Between Havana and Pinar del Rio on the eastern part of the Guaniguanico mountain range is the Las Terrazas agricultural community designed by Mario Girona and built in 1967. This 12,500-acre working community is part of the Sierra del Rosario Reserve and was designated a UNESCO biosphere reserve in 1984. One of the most interesting aspects of the biosphere reserve is its link with coffee, as it is the site of the first significant coffee plantation in the New World. In 1791 French immigrants fled Haiti's slave rebellion and established over fifty coffee plantations in the area. Cafetal Buenavista is the only estate that is fully reconstructed, where the early coffee drying terraces, machinery, and techniques are preserved—and the home-brewed coffee is outstanding.

To reach the island's westernmost points, Cabo de San Antonio and Punta Cajón, one has to travel along the Península de Guanahacabibes. It is one of Cuba's largest natural reserves and was declared a UNESCO biosphere reserve in 1987. The reserve is diverse, with evergreen and semi-deciduous forests, marshlands, pastures, mangroves, coastal scrublands, and a pure silica white-sand plain, plus more than one hundred lakes. This peninsula was one of the last refuges of the island's indigenous people as they attempted to escape the brutal Spanish conquistadors.

64 | ORQUIDEARIO DE SOROA

Located in the UNESCO biosphere reserve Sierra del Rosario, this is thought to be the world's largest orchid garden with more than 20,000 plants and 800 species of orchids, 250 of which are endemic (left and above). Created in 1943 by a Spaniard, it is presently maintained by the University of Pinar del Río. Nearby is the San Juan waterfall (opposite).

65 | PINAR DEL RÍO

Pinar del Río was founded in 1669. It was settled by tobacco farmers and prospered because of the profitable tobacco trade. The town and surrounding region is Cuba's center for the cultivation, production, and processing of tobacco. Uncontested, the world's finest tobacco is grown in this area. An example of Pinar del Río's esoteric architecture is the Palacio de Guasch with its unusual Gothic, Moorish, and baroque decorative façade (opposite). Don't forget to try the local Guayabita del Pinar (above), a spicy alcohol libation based on a secret recipe and derived from a kind of guava berry that grows only in the mountains around Pinar del Río.

Diverse and dissimilar architecture can be found throughout the city (above), and visitors should stop in the elegant neoclassical gem José Jacinto Milanés Theater, where performances and lectures are regularly scheduled (opposite).

66 | FINCA AGROECOLÓGICA EL PARAÍSO

El Paraíso near the outskirts of Viñales village is a family-run private restaurant (*paladar*) managed by Rachel García. García's establishment is legendary for serving a secret-recipe "anti-stress" piña colada–like cocktail. The ingredients include Cuban white rum, coconut milk, mint, basil, anise, and other unnamed herbs (opposite). One of the many bed-and-breakfast establishments that line the streets of Viñales village and can be booked through Airbnb (above).

67 | TOBACCO FARMS

Planting, growing, and harvesting tobacco is labor intensive and mostly done by hand (top left). The tobacco flower blooms for only a short time and the seeds are used to start another plant (bottom left). The late Alejandro Robaina's tobacco farm is now run by his grandson Hirochi Robaina, who is as graciously welcoming to visitors as his grandfather was. The Robaina farm is in Cuba's Vuelta Abajo tobacco region near the town of San Luis outside Pinar del Río and it is the only Cuban grower with a cigar bearing its name (opposite). **OVERLEAF:** Another interesting tobacco farm to visit is Benito Camejo's farm on the outskirts of Viñales, where the tobacco growing process is described step by step. In his A-frame drying barn (right), Camejo rolls cigars (left), and afterward he invites visitors into his home for cups of locally grown coffee with liquid sugar (white rum).

68 | CAFETAL BUENAVISTA

Cafetal Buenavista is a restored coffee plantation established in 1801 after French immigrants fled Haiti following the early 1790s revolution (above). The preserved stone terraces are where coffee beans were laid to dry and at the top of the terraces is an ox-powered coffee grinder (opposite).

69 | LAS TERRAZAS

Las Terrazas derives its name from the terraces laid out for the pine, teak, cedar, and mahogany trees that were planted in the late 1960s and early 1970s. Declared a UNESCO biosphere reserve, this ecotourism village and working community is situated on a peaceful man-made lake and provides comprehensive workshop programs, hiking, horseback riding, zip-line canopy tours, boat and water activities, and camping (opposite and above).

70 | MOGOTES

OVERLEAF: The *mogotes* of the Viñales Valley offer one of the world's foremost spectacular, bizarre, and unique landscapes. Shaped like tree- and brush-covered haystacks or sugar loaves, these large limestone hills are said to be the oldest ancient rock formations in Cuba. Visitors can spend days investigating the largest network of caves in the Caribbean, hiking the red earth tobacco fields, and rock climbing the limestone formations, in addition to wandering and exploring the nearby village of Viñales.

71 | RUISEÑOR VALLEY

At the northern border of Viñales Valley is Ancón Valley, a place untouched by tourism and difficult to find. This unspoiled and rarely visited valley is only the starting point from which to hike and find a camouflaged cave entrance (top and bottom left). After a twenty-minute trek through the cave (impossible without a flashlight), one arrives at Cuba's prettiest hidden valley, Ruiseñor, a sixty- to seventy-acre valley referred to locally as the "Secret Valley," where both Amerindians in the sixteenth century and enslaved runaway workers (maroons) in the eighteenth century hid from their persecutors (opposite).

CHAPTER 5

HAVANA

Cuba's NOBLE *City*

Traveling around Cuba for fifteen years, I've learned that there are two Cubas: Havana and everywhere that is not Havana. This city is one of a kind. Havana (Habana in Spanish) was settled in 1519 and has been the island's capital since 1607. It was proclaimed a UNESCO World Heritage site in 1982 and will celebrate its five-hundredth anniversary in 2019. Havana has slowly but steadily been preparing to celebrate this historic event for the past decade by restoring many of its buildings.

Havana is best known for its colonial past and there are literally hundreds of historically significant streets and structures in the city. The first structures the Spanish built were fortifications, based on medieval and Renaissance designs, and many of those still stand. Following the dictates of Spain's Phillip II, who promulgated the Laws

of the Indies, sixteenth-century Spanish architects and engineers adopted the grid-based plan with each set of streets organized around a central plaza. Typically, a central plaza would be bordered by military headquarters on one side, a gubernatorial residence and offices on another, a cathedral or church on the third, and military officers' quarters and barracks on the fourth. In Old Havana, the majority of the domestic buildings were constructed in the Spanish baroque style, modified to account for the tropical climate with high ceilings, heavy window shutters and doors, verandas, and arcades.

There are hundreds of beautiful and interesting places to visit in Havana, and it would be impossible to list them all. Indeed, one of the most enjoyable things to do in Havana is to wander through the neighborhoods in the older section of the city and simply gaze upon the architecture. A good starting point for this kind of stroll would be the Plaza de la Catedral and the recently restored seventeenth-century Palacio de los Condes de Casa Bayona, which was built in the Renaissance style and is now Havana's Museo de Arte Colonial. Directly across the plaza is the city's main cathedral, begun in 1748, completed in 1777, and Cuba's best example of the ornamental Churrigueresque Cuban baroque style. The façade of this cathedral was described by Cuban author Alejo Carpentier as "music turned into stone."

In the eighteenth century, Havana's domestic architecture became even more opulent, combining elements of colonial baroque and Mudéjar with the newly emerging neoclassical style. One of the finest examples of stylistically transitional baroque and neoclassicism is the Palacio de los Generales on Plaza de Armas. Construction on the palace began in 1773 and

PREVIOUS SPREAD: Near Havana's capital at the head of Parque de la Fraternidad is a Carrara marble fountain known as the Fuente de la India, or La Noble Habana, an allegorical representation and symbol of Cuba's capital city. The Amerindian maiden holds a cornucopia and a shield bearing the arms of Havana.

OPPOSITE, RIGHT, AND OVERLEAF: The citizens of Havana (Habaneros) are sophisticated, learned, courteous, and generous people. From an early age, children learn all of these qualities, plus a deep respect for achievement, whether in sports, dance, music, or art. Although Havana has suffered decades of neglect, the city resembles an abandoned stage set, and habaneros will always take the time to help those in need.

was completed in 1791, and it then served as a residence for the governor and his family. On the same plaza is the Palacio del Segundo Cabo. Built as a private home in 1776, it became the vice governor's residence. Both of these grand palacios were designed and built by Cuban architect and engineer Antonio Fernández de Trebejos y Zaldívar, and they share a similar look. Two other plazas worth a visit are Plaza de San Francisco de Asís and Plaza Vieja. But again, there are literally hundreds of colonial palaces, mansions, castles, shops, galleries, cafés, restaurants, and music venues in Havana itself and in the areas surrounding the city, and almost all of them warrant a visit. It's impossible to go wrong.

In addition to the riches offered by Havana's centuries of history, the city has numerous twentieth-century sites unique to Cuba. Most of Havana was built in the fifty-seven years that stretched from independence in 1902 to the revolution in 1959. Two of the best known and most illustrious examples of early twentieth-century architecture in the city are the social and mutual-aid society clubs that reflected and legitimized the wealth of Havana's late-nineteenth- and early twentieth-century elites. The Galician Center was built in 1915 to accommodate Havana's community from Spain's northwestern province of Galicia. Recently renamed the Alicia Alonso Grand Theater, it now is home to Cuba's world-famous national ballet company. On the opposite side of Central Park stands the Centro Asturiano, built in 1927 for Spaniards from the northern coastal province of Asturia. That building now houses the international art collection of the Museo Nacional de Bellas Artes.

The majority of Havana's large twentieth-century private residences built before the 1959 revolution were nationalized after being abandoned by owners who left the island. One exception is the Beaux Arts home of my friend Jossie Alonso, who welcomes photographers (Annie Leibovitz photographed pop singer Rihanna here). Jossie has lived in her house in the suburb of Verdado since it was built in the late 1920s.

During the twentieth century, a wide array of modern and contemporary hotels was built in Havana. Three of the most interesting are the Hotel Nacional de Cuba that opened on New Year's Day in 1930; the mobster-owned Hotel Habana Riviera that opened in 1957; and the twenty-seven-story, 630-room former Havana Hilton that became the Hotel Habana Libre. All three have their original interiors and are still in operation—visiting them is like traveling back in time. The same could be said of a visit to the Tropicana Club, where dancers and singers have performed for more than sixty years.

A previous era is also evoked by the lobby of the opulent French-inspired Art Deco Bacardi building. Completed in 1930, it has colorful enameled terracotta panels of nude nymphs by Maxfield Parrish (his muse, Susan Lewin, was the model). Blocks away, the Paseo del Prado, Havana's most picturesque tree-lined boulevard, begins at the Capitol and ends at the Malecón, a seaside promenade overlooking the Straits of Florida. Outside Havana sits Museo Hemingway or Finca Vigía (Lookout Farm), Ernest Hemingway's home for nearly twenty-two years.

The kitchen and dining room of a Havana neighborhood home still occupied by one of the
original owners, Jossie Alonso, who welcomes photographers to use her house as a backdrop.
Vanity Fair magazine photographer Annie Leibovitz shot pop music star Rihanna here.

Among other architectural standouts is the Museo Nacional de Bellas Artes (National Museum of Fine Arts) of Havana, built in 1954, which houses the world's finest collection of Wifredo Lam paintings. Another phenomenal example of mid-twentieth-century architecture is provided by the National Art Schools (Escuelas Nacionales de Arte, now known as the Instituto Superior de Arte) designed by Cuban architect Ricardo Porro and Italian architects Roberto Gottardi and Vittorio Garatti in 1961. The five art schools were built on an expropriated country club golf course on orders from Fidel Castro who said the school should be designed to be "the most beautiful academy of arts in the whole world."

Oscar Wilde once said, "Art is the most intense mode of individualism that the world has known." Today, Cuba's artists are paving the path to change on the island. Though younger artists are often less overtly political than the members of previous generations, many of Cuba's most prominent contemporary artists—Kcho, Tomás Sánchez, Manuel Mendive, and Carlos Garaicoa—are strongly influenced by their Cuban roots. Established and emerging painters, sculptors, and conceptual artists are producing like gangbusters to meet demand as foreign art collectors flock to the island. Since the mid-1980s, the Havana Art Biennial has attracted modern art collectors and museums. And while private art galleries were once illegal, a recent change in the law has opened up the art market dramatically. Some of the leading emerging young painters are brothers Kadir and Kelvin López, Miguel Machado, and Ketty Rodriguez, in addition to the artists that exhibit at the Fábrica de Arte Cubano (FAC), a gallery and performance space in a former cooking-oil factory in Havana's Vedado neighborhood. Concerts, film, art exhibitions, and other events are staged at FAC as well.

That's far from the only place visitors can enjoy a show: Music and dance events are widely available to the visiting public in Cuba these days; even the rituals of Santería, an Afro-Cuban religion, are accessible to tourists. These once-sacred rituals have evolved into performances—many of them squarely aimed at tourists, but interesting nonetheless.

Havana isn't just about art and architecture; there are countless music venues and museums, paladares with wonderful cuisine, parks and botanical gardens, and world class dance performances. In addition to the Cuban clichés of tourist markets, antique cars, captivating cabarets, carnivals and nightlife, the best tobacco and rum in the world is available for the asking. Any visitor can stay busy weeks at a time or even better, for multiple visits. Havana is a city sealed against time for more than fifty years and now with the eased restrictions on travel to the island and the change in laws on the island, the irrepressible cultural vibrancy of the city is attracting hordes of visitors.

One of the thousands of hidden surprises of Havana is the Parque John Lennon (John Lennon Park) in Havana's Vedado neighborhood. At the foot of the bench where a bronze sculpture of Lennon sits is an inscription from Lennon's song *Imagine* that reads, "Dices que soy un soñador /pero no soy el único" (You may say I'm a dreamer /But I'm not the only one). Lennon's verse continues, "I hope some day you'll join us /And the world will be as one."

OPPOSITE: The Beatles were very popular in Cuba, and Parque John Lennon is one of more than one hundred parks and plazas in Havana. Vigils are still held here on December 8, the anniversary of Lennon's death.

OVERLEAF: Havana at night is as alive as any modern city today, but the nightlife and entertainment are usually found in secluded, sometimes isolated places. Music and performing venues can be discovered in hidden courtyards, as well as on flashy cabaret stages.

72 | MUSEO DE ARTES DECORATIVAS

Built in 1926 by a sugar magnate, this Vedado mansion
was given to the original owner's daughter, who
allegedly considered it too ostentatious and passed
it on to her aunt, the Countess of Revilla de Camargo.
The double-height entrance hall leads to one of the
most beautiful residential staircases in Cuba (opposite).
Today, the house is Havana's Museum of Decorative
Arts, with a collection of French period furniture,
important paintings, and porcelain, silver, and gold
tableware and cutlery.

73 | MUSEO NAPOLEÓNICO

The finest and most extensive collection of Napoleonic memorabilia outside of Paris is exhibited in Havana's Napoleon Museum, once the home of Cuban politician Orestes Ferrara before it was nationalized and designated a museum (above). The actual collection belonged to Cuban sugar king Julio Lobo.

74 | UNIVERSIDAD DE LA HABANA

Across from the Napoleon Museum is the University of Havana, a building with a neoclassical façade at the top of an eighty-eight-step stairway that reminds many of NYC's Columbia University (opposite). This stairway has been the scene of numerous student protests and the campus was once considered a hotbed of student radicalism.

TEMPLO BETH - SHALOM GRAN SINAGOGA DE LA COMUNIDAD HEBREA DE CUBA

During the first half of the twentieth century, the development of modern Havana accomplished unprecedented achievements in urban planning and infrastructure in both civil and domestic architecture. The largest part of Havana was built in the fifty-seven years from independence in 1902 to the mid-twentieth century revolution in 1959. Two of the hundreds of modern buildings in Havana are the Hebrew Community Building built in 1953 (left) and the American Embassy completed in 1952 (opposite), both in the Vedado neighborhood.

76 | OLD HAVANA

The area known as Old Havana (La Habana Vieja) is the oldest part of the colonial city and has literally hundreds of important and historically significant sites. It takes the best part of a week to really appreciate all the hidden venues, the antique monumental buildings, the plazas, harbor, and parks that should all be seen. There are countless cafés, bars, studios, galleries, museums, churches, palacios, forts, shops, and restaurants to experience.

77 | CASA DE LA OBRAPÍA

The doorway and interior courtyard of the
1660s residence Casa de la Obrapía, one of
the jewels of Cuban baroque architecture,
is on one of the side streets in Old Havana
(left and opposite). The stonework for the
door was executed in Cádiz, Spain in the late
1600s and shipped to Havana.

78 | CENTRAL HAVANA

Bordering Old Havana are the neighborhoods of Central Havana that include El Prado, Central Park, the Capitolio, museums, grand elegant old hotels, homes, and commercial buildings like the Partagás cigar factory (opposite) and the art deco Bacardí building. The Palace of Fine Arts (left) built in 1954 is dedicated solely to Cuban art and boasts the finest collection of Cuban art in the world. Among the thousands of paintings is *I Don't Want to Go to Heaven* by Augusto García Menocal (above). It tells the story of the Taíno leader Hatuey who had been captured and was about to be burned at the stake when he was asked by a priest if he wanted to go to heaven. Hatuey replied with a question of his own: "Will those white men go to heaven?" After the priest responded, "Yes," Hatuey replied, "If they will be there then no, I don't want to go to heaven."

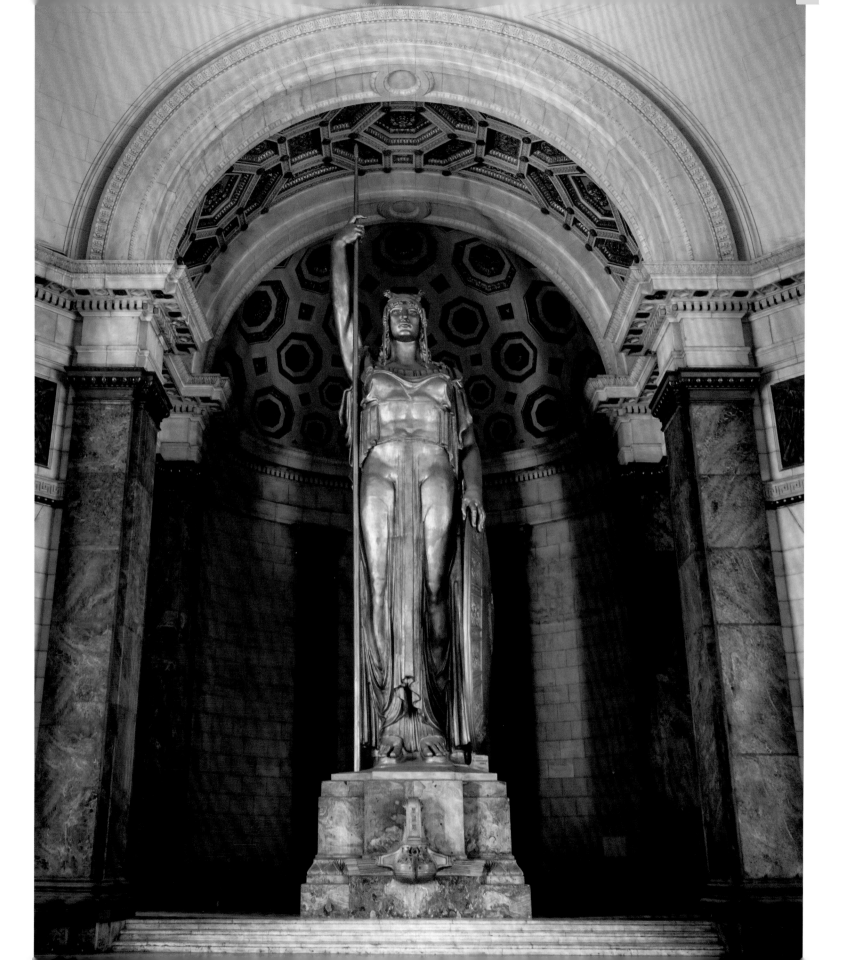

El Capitolio (above), Cuba's national capitol building, was completed in 1929 and was inspired by the U.S. Capitol in Washington, D.C. The statue of the Republic (La Estatua de la República) is bronze covered in gold leaf and at 50 feet high is the world's third tallest statue under cover (opposite).

79 | **VEDADO**

The giant Y-shaped luxury apartment building, FOCSA, dominated the Vedado neighborhood and was the second tallest concrete building in the world when it was built in 1956 (left).

Also completed in the mid-1950s was the José Martí Memorial that looms over Plaza de la Revolución (left). The twenty-one-story Mafia-owned Hotel Habana Riviera that opened in 1958 was Havana's first hotel with central air conditioning (top right) and is located on the Malecón, the city's serpentine shorefront drive where Habaneros of all ages are drawn to watch the sunset, children come to swim, and lovers meet (bottom right).

80 | PLAZA DE SAN FRANCISCO

This plaza is filled with architecture that spans more than three hundred years (opposite). The baroque church Basílica Menor de San Francisco de Asís, with its porticoed gallery (above); rooms of the Franciscan monastery are adjacent to the church, which today is used for chamber music recitals, lectures, and concerts.

8I | PLAZA DE LA CATEDRAL

The cathedral of Havana, the dominating building on this beautiful old plaza, was built in the mid-1700s and dedicated to Christopher Columbus. The exuberant rhythmic, scrolled, and undulating façade makes it the quintessential example of Cuban baroque architecture. It was described by celebrated Cuban author Alejo Carpentier as "music turned into stone." **OVERLEAF:** The early eighteenth-century facade of Casa del Conde de Casa Bayona on Plaza de la Catedral (right). A view from the Casa del Conde de Bayona, now the Museo de Arte Colonial (Havana's Museum of Colonial Art) that houses a collection of eighteenth-and-nineteenth-century Cuban furniture and decorative arts (left).

CUBA: 101 BEAUTIFUL & NOSTALGIC PLACES TO VISIT

82 | PLAZA DE ARMAS

The oldest of Havana's plazas, the Plaza de Armas, is where the city was first established nearly five hundred years ago and is surrounded by historically significant buildings. The Casa del Conde de Santovenia, now the Hotel Santa Isabel, was a family home built in 1784 and later purchased by the Count of Santovenia (opposite). The book market (above) is Cuba's largest secondhand market for books, maps, posters, and antique knickknacks. OVERLEAF: Two of Cuba's greatest and most awesome residential palaces built in the 1700s, the Palacio de los Capitanes Generales (left) and Palacio del Segundo Cabo (right), are located on the plaza and are well worth exploring.

83 | PLAZA VIEJA

The Old Plaza (opposite) was originally planned and laid out in 1559 and both residential and commercial buildings that span a three-hundred-year period surround the plaza. These include my favorite café, Café El Escorial, where Cuba's superlative, second-to-none coffee is served and a traveler is lucky to have the chance to purchase a bag of this delicious coffee. Hint: Get there in the morning before it's all gone.

84 | PRESIDENTIAL PALACE

OVERLEAF: The Presidential Palace has been renamed the Museo de la Revolución. The building was first conceived in Cuba centuries before work began, and work on it continued throughout the first half of the twentieth century (left). It is an iconic example of monumentality, presently filled with photographs, documents, uniforms, weapons, and memorabilia featuring Cuba's struggle for independence. The lavish neoclassical architectural bones of the building haven't been lost, nor has the classical and sophisticated interior design with decorations by Tiffany (right).

85 | FÁBRICA DE ARTE CUBANO

One of Havana's newest nighttime venues, FAC, is a hip chic nightspot housed in a former cooking oil factory and warehouse with landmark chimney (opposite). There is *siempre un montón de todo* (always a lot of everything) happening here on the weekends, with three different music stages (bottom right), revolving art exhibitions, film, dance, theater, fashion shows, and performance art. To add to the fun and enjoyment there is a particularly good paladar, El Cocinero, with a rooftop dining area located underneath the factory's imposing brick chimney (top right).

86 | HOTEL NACIONAL DE CUBA

This hotel opened on New Year's Day 1930 and was built on Havana's beautiful seaside boulevard, the Malecón (opposite). Hotel Nacional was immortalized in the movie *The Godfather Part II* and served as a backdrop for the factually documented and infamous 1946 gangster summit, the Havana Conference, a historic meeting of the U.S. Mafia and Sicilian Cosa Nostra members. The hotel's guest book includes everyone of note from the era: Josephine Baker, Marlene Dietrich, Rita Hayworth, Ava Gardner, Frank Sinatra, Gary Cooper, Errol Flynn, Winston Churchill, Marlon Brando, and many, many more.

87 | CASTILLO DEL MORRO

OVERLEAF: Construction of the fort and lighthouse Castillo del Morro, located at the entrance to Havana Bay, began in 1589 to dissuade Spain's enemies, especially pirates, from approaching the city. A collection of flags from different countries is kept in the harbormaster's office and quarters (bottom left). The original American-flagged tall ship *Roseway* is pictured passing the lighthouse in the fall of 2016 (right). *Roseway* was the first original authentic American tall ship to enter the bay of Havana in fifty-nine years. Every evening at exactly 9:00 p.m. a traditional theatrical cannon ceremony is held, representing a salute to the historical time that alerted all city citizens that the harbor entrance and city gates were closing (top left).

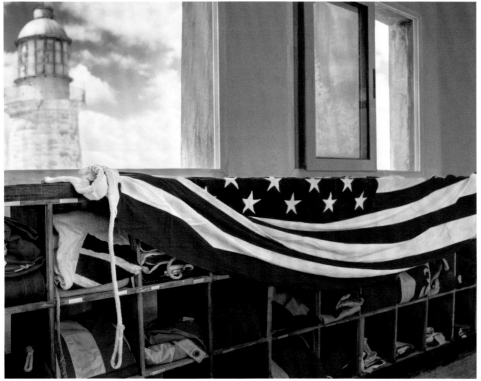

88 | ESCUELA NACIONAL DE ARTES

Havana's National School of Arts (opposite) was built at Fidel Castro's behest and assigned to the late Cuban architect Ricardo Porro, who was asked to gather a team of architects with the purpose of designing and building "the most beautiful art school in the world." Only two, fine arts and modern dance, of the original five intended schools (fine arts, drama, music, modern dance, and ballet) continue to function today. Miguel Machado (top right) and Ketty Rodríguez (bottom right) are recent graduates of the school. The award-winning documentary film *Unfinished Spaces* tells the compelling story of the creation, neglect, closing, and resurrection of the schools.

89 | FINCA VIGÍA

OVERLEAF: Ernest Hemingway moved to Cuba in 1939 and spent twenty-one years at Finca Vigía (Lookout Farm), which was originally built in 1887 in the suburb of San Francisco de Paula, approximately ten miles southeast of Havana. Discovered and rented by Hemingway's third wife, Martha Gellhorn, Finca Vigía has interiors that have been kept exactly as they were in 1960 when Hemingway departed Cuba for the summer months with his fourth wife, Mary Welsh, thinking they would return months later. This is the only authentic Hemingway living museum in the world.

90 | FUSTER TILE PARK

Ceramic artist José Fuster, nicknamed the "Picasso of the Caribbean," has an open-air studio gallery at his home, a surreal world made of colorful broken tiles (above). This outsider type of art expression is childlike and inspired mostly by city and farmyard scenes (opposite). Fuster's son now joins him in his work, which presently covers the entire neighborhood, including the city bus stop blocks away from his house.

91 | LA GUARIDA PALADAR

La Guarida paladar has been open more than twenty years but continues to be Havana's most sought-after reservation. This privately owned paladar operates out of Enrique del Valle and his wife's former home, on the third floor of a dilapidated Havana tenement building and the setting of the Oscar-nominated Cuban film *Fresa y Chocolate (Strawberry and Chocolate).* Shown here are the new rooftop bar (opposite) and the private humidor and cigar bar smoking room (above).

92 | ANTIQUES SHOPS

Since laws and regulations in Cuba have loosened up, many small businesses, studios, galleries, and shops have opened: t-shirt design shops, vanity galleries selling the owner's art and/or handicrafts, takeout pizza shops where the food is served out the front door of a private home, and antiques shops. This shop, next to Sloppy Joe's Bar, Memorias (Memories), carries an array of old and interesting items for sale (above). Another attractive and compelling design gallery nearby that should not be missed is Clandestina.

93 | KCHO STUDIO

The private studio/gallery of Cuba's distinguished artist Alexis Leiva Machado, better known as Kcho, is now open by appointment to visitors (opposite). Alongside his studio compound, Kcho has created a nonprofit multi-cultural community complex that serves local residents. All age groups are welcomed into the assistance programs and different project spaces.

94 | CEMETERY CRISTÓBAL COLÓN

This cemetery was designed, laid out, and built from the 1870s through the 1880s. It is the largest cemetery in the Americas and is by far one the world's most impressive collections of flamboyant funerary architecture, counting more than five hundred important vaults, mausoleums, and chapels and thousands of tombstones. Cuba's most prominent and luminary figures, including artists, writers, rebellion leaders, politicians, and celebrities, are buried here.

95 | LA VIRGEN DE REGLA

After a ten-minute ferry ride across Havana Bay ends at the foot of the seventeenth-century town of Regla, known for its strong Afro-Cuban culture, and after a five-minute walk from the shore to the village church, Nuestra Señora de la Virgen de Regla (opposite), where the Virgin of Regla, patron saint of fishermen, is enshrined in a side altar (top left), one begins to have a better understanding of the devotion to and seriousness of religion in Cuba. Devotees of the Santería religion are sometimes found outside the church soliciting and telling followers' fortunes (bottom left).

96 | LOS JARDINES DE LA TROPICAL

The owner of the popular brand of beer La Tropical built Tropical Gardens on the banks of Havana's Almendares River at the turn of the twentieth century (above). In its heyday, Tropical Gardens, which resembles the Alhambra, was a gathering place for high society, where the most popular orchestras played while people danced in the ballroom (opposite). Although it has deteriorated, dance festivals and rock concerts are sometimes still scheduled here.

97 | MUSEO DEL RON HAVANA CLUB

For more than 100 years, Cuba has been famous for its rum and rum cocktail concoctions: Mojitos, Cuba Libres, Havana Especiales, and Daiquiris. One of the most convenient and outstanding haunts to try all of these is the Museum of Rum (Museo del Ron) and its adjoining barroom where live music and excellent cocktails are always served (above and opposite).

98 | FUNDACIÓN ANTONIO NÚÑEZ JIMÉNEZ

The Foundation of Nature and Man was founded in 1994 by the late anthropologist, explorer, and intellectual Antonio Núñez Jiménez, whose daughter, Liliana Núñez, is presently the director (above). This foundation and small and rewarding museum is a non-governmental, nonprofit organization that continues the legacy of its founder through programs of research and development activities that promote the cultural values of nature and the environment. The museum exhibits artifacts from Núñez Jiménez's 1987 11,000-mile canoe trip from the Amazon River's source to the ocean and fascinating ephemera from the founder's life's work.

99 | PALADAR LA COCINA DE LILLIAM

This is unquestionably the greatest garden paladar in Havana (opposite). Chef Lilliam Domínguez Palenzuela begins cooking early every morning to fulfill the desires of her diners each night with home-cooked Cuban nouvelle cuisine. The lush, romantically lit garden adjoins Domínguez Palenzuela's home, where she first opened her restaurant more than twenty years ago.

IOO | TEATRO MARTÍ

The 1884 theater has recently been restored to its original grandeur and elegance and features programs, including dance, plays, operas, and musical performances. The sophisticated and tasteful interior consists of extraordinary ironwork and creates perfect acoustics (opposite). Cuba's historically significant constitution for the republic was signed here in 1901.

IOI | GRAN TEATRO

OVERLEAF: Havana's Grand Theater has recently been renamed the Gran Teatro de La Habana Alicia Alonso to commemorate the Cuban prima ballerina assoluta Alicia Alonso (left and right). The original theater, named Tacón, was built in 1838 and in 1914 the monumental palace for the Centro Gallego was built in the same place, surrounding the original theater. The palace was built for the Cuban Galician Community, an affluent Spanish leisure club. The famous Sarah Bernhardt performed here, as did Arthur Rubinstein and Andrés Segovia.

ACKNOWLEDGMENTS

This is my fifth book with Rizzoli Publications and I would first like to thank Marco Ausenda, Rizzoli's President and CEO, for recognizing the importance of Cuba today, and Charles Miers, Publisher, for his support and encouragement throughout this project, and my editor, Ellen Cohen for her guidance, patience, and gentle but pertinacious persistence to submit my work on time.

I also sincerely thank my team, especially the remarkably talented photographer, Jorge A. Laserna who indefatigably labored with me for two years traveling throughout the entire island of Cuba, often to very remote areas. My heartfelt thankfulness goes out to Mónica Fernández for her scholarly research and unwavering dedication to seeing that all Spanish translations were correct and to Karolina Stefanski for her organizational skills and beautifully appointed styling. My deep gratitude goes out to Barbara Cameron Gregg for the hours she volunteered to spend at the tedious task of proofreading and my wholehearted appreciation to Susi Oberhelman for her creativity and amazing design talents.

Finally I am deeply grateful to all my Cuban friends who pointed me in the right direction and helped identify the sometimes hidden but always important and beautiful places to visit in Cuba. It is impossible to list them all and I apologize to those who I have failed to mention by name but please know I am indebted to you for your gracious hospitality and for sharing the unforgettable experience that Cuba has to offer. Special appreciation and thanks go to: Dr. Eusebio Leal, Havana City Historian; Sonia Ortega, Vice Dean of International Relationship at the National Art Schools; Ambassador Jeffrey DeLaurentis the Chargé d'Affaires at the U.S. Embassy in Havana, Cuba; David Guggenheim, President Director, Cuba Conservancy and his organization Ocean Doctor for tutoring me on the importance of Cuba's reef ecosystem and his amazing underwater photography; Maria de Lourdes Duke and her organization, Fundación Amistad, whose mission it is to foster mutual understanding and respect between the peoples of the U.S. and Cuba; Marta Castellanos and Remberto Ramirez; Brent Winebrenner, May Reguera, Joel Guerra and Jorge García for the photographs they contributed; Thomas and Andy Connors for their instructive council; Liliana Núñez Velis, President of the Fundación Antonio Núñez Jiménez; José Rodríguez Barreras, Camagüey City Historian; Joel Jover and his wife Ileana Sánchez; Margarita (Maggie) Alarcón Perea; Ada Rosa Alfonso and Isbel Ferreiro director and deputy director of the Hemingway Museum in Havana; Ramon Guilarte; Hirochi Robania; Benito Camejo; Rachel García; Jossie Alonso; Miguel Machado; Ketty Rodríguez; Alexis (Kcho) Leiva Machado; Carlos Mata; Lilliam Domínguez Palenzuela; Enrique del Valle and Augusto (Kiko) Villalón.

All photography is by Jorge A. Laserna except on the following pages:
Michael Connors: 16 (top left), 76-77, 234; Darwin Davidson: 22 (top right); Joel Guerra: 72, 273 (bottom), 276 (bottom), 277, 286;
David Guggenheim: 130, 136-37, 138 (top and bottom); May Reguera: 296; Brent Winebrenner: 44, 192, 193, 229, 250 (left), 253, 262, 263, 303, 304

First published in the United States of America in 2017 by
Rizzoli International Publications, Inc. • 300 Park Avenue South • New York, NY 10010 • www.rizzoliusa.com

Editor: Ellen R. Cohen • Designed by Susi Oberhelman

ISBN: 978-0-8478-5840-8 • Library of Congress Control Number: 2017940513

Copyright © 2017 Michael Connors

Printed in China

2017 2018 2019 2020 2021 / 10 9 8 7 6 5 4 3 2 1

PAGES 2-3: The remote, arid, and dramatically scenic eastern shore road from Guantánamo to Santiago de Cuba.
PAGES 4-5: The fishing boats of Casilda, a village on the Caribbean coast, five miles from Trinidad.
PAGE 6: Besides all the beautiful places in Cuba, the island has the natural beauty of the human spirit that is expressed as *Cubanía* (Cubanness).
PAGES 8-9: A typical example of Cuban innovation for solving the transportation problem that plagues the country.

CARTE RÉDUITE
DE L'ISLE DE CUBE
Dressée au Dépôt des Cartes et Plans de la Marine
POUR LE SERVICE DES VAISSEAUX DU ROY
Par ordre de M. LE DUC DE CHOISEUL
Colonel général des Suisses et Grisons
Ministre de la Guerre et de la Marine
Par le S. Bellin Ingénieur de la Marine et du
Dépôt des Plans, Censeur Royal de l'Académie
de Marine et de la Société Royale de Londres
M.DCC.LXII
Echelles

Havana
Matanzas
Remedio
Pinar del Rio
Cienfuegos
Trinidad
Ville du S.
Isla de la Juventud
Isle de Pin
Les Jardins
Jardines de la Reina
Cap S.
Antoine
Cayman Brac
Petit Cayman
Route